QUALIF

WHY GOOD MEN REMAIN SINGLE

Dwayne L. Buckingham, Ph.D., LCSW, BCD

Other Great Books by Dr. Dwayne L. Buckingham

A Phenomenological Study of the Experiences of Black Women

Can Black Women Achieve Marital Satisfaction?
How Childhood Nurturing Experiences Impact Marital Happiness

Unconditional Love:
What Every Woman and Man Desires in a Relationship

A Black Man's Worth: Conqueror and Head of Household

A Black Woman's Worth: My Queen and Backbone

Groundbreaking Films by Dr. Dwayne L. Buckingham

A Black Man's Worth: Conqueror and Head of Household

A Black Woman's Worth: My Queen and Backbone

Qualified, yet Single: Why Good Men Remain Single

www.drbuckingham.com

QUALIFIED, YET SINGLE

WHY GOOD MEN REMAIN SINGLE

Dwayne L. Buckingham, Ph.D., LCSW, BCD

An Imprint of RHCS Publishers

Qualified, yet Single

To protect the confidentially and privacy of individuals who have shared their stories, identifiable information has been modified.

All books by Dr. Buckingham are available at special quantity discounts for sales, promotions, fundraising and educational purposes. For details and to order additional copies of this book, please visit: www.realhorizonsdlb.com or write to:

R.E.A.L. Horizons Consulting Service, LLC
P.O. Box 2665
Silver Spring, MD 20915
240-242-4087 Voice mail
www.drbuckingham.com

FIRST EDITION

Design by Stephen Future

Library of Congress Control Number: 2011962627

ISBN: 978-0-9849423-4-3

Edited by Sue Morris

For Worldwide Distribution

Printed in the United States of America

Dedication

To every single woman who desires marriage
but struggles to secure long-term companionship.

Message to Single Good Women

You are worthy of receiving whatever your heart desires, but remember that a man can only treat you bad or disrespectfully if you allow him to. Time after time, some of you complain about how men are no good dogs who are preoccupied with conquering women. As you reflect on your view of men, commitment and relationships, stop to ask yourself if you are a good judge of character. The easiest way to judge the men you choose to interact with is to look at yourself. Do you possess qualities that are needed to be in a healthy relationship? Are you truly ready for commitment? Do you have any unresolved emotional shortcomings? As you take this educational journey with me, I encourage you to look at yourself. Remember that entering into and sustaining a healthy relationship is only possible if two people are willing to reflect on and address their own emotional shortcomings.

Message to Single Good Men

The good guy persona does not give you the right to play games with women. I realize that you want and desire companionship, but I encourage you to show women respect by letting them go if you are not truly interested. Many of you think that it is okay to feel a woman out before you commit. This is acceptable; however, most of you have a good idea from day one whether or not a woman will make the cut. With this in mind, do not engage a woman if you have issues with her or have failed to deal with your own issues.

Qualified, yet Single

If you are attractive, I will tell you what you want to hear
But please do not listen too close because you might hear my fear.

Leading you on is not difficult to do
Because you are like a broken table and I am the glue.

I shine on the outside so you can't see through
But underneath the façade my heart is cold and blue.

You think I am the one so you don't mind the wait
And have convinced yourself to believe that what we have is fate.

I tell you I want to be with you because you are great
Open up your eyes woman, most men use the same bait.

I have great qualifications that you might like,
But everything that looks good on the outside is not right.

I tell you I care, but will not let you near
But you continue to hold on like I am some kind of souvenir.

If you want to find true love, pay attention to what you hear
Because good men like myself will not commit until we conquer our fear.

Take Home Messages:

Qualifications do not mean qualified!
Behind every behavior there is an emotion!

Acknowledgments

I would like to acknowledge and thank all the men who provided insight and shared their personal views and stories about commitment, women and relationships.

To my sisters Linda, Alma, Cynthia, and Bonnie for helping me develop the fortitude to treat women with respect and dignity as I ventured into manhood.

To my God-mother, Eugenia, I am appreciative of the ongoing support you provide in my quest to understand and do right by women.

To my dear friends LaNetra Kellar and Jennifer Jones, who spent numerous hours and days talking to me about women and challenged me to explore and process my fears as a single man. Our conversations ignited a flame in me that served as the foundation for writing this book.

To women all around the world, you all have not given up on love despite the emotional and physical challenges you all face at the hands of men on a daily basis. I truly appreciate the strength and courage you all display in regards to putting your hearts on the line. Thanks for encouraging me to do right and I am truly sorry if I have hurt any of you.

Glossary of Terms

Qualifications: Qualities that make single men suitable for relationships include financially stable, focused, driven, successful and family oriented.

Qualified Men: Men who possess certain personal and/or professional attributes that women find attractive and appealing.

Good Men: Men who are desirable in nature because they are kind, thoughtful, easy going, good hearted, honest, giving, open-minded and considerate.

A Jump-Off: A woman who gives of herself sexually without wanting much in return. She is easily persuaded and impressed with a man's outwardly appearance, status and verbal presentation.

Emotionally Unavailable Men: Men who do not share their inner feelings, thoughts or desires. They desire and seek companionship, but do not invest emotionally.

Fear: A debilitating and anxiety-provoking emotion that triggers a fight or flight response.

Contents

PREFACE

INTRODUCTION

---

1 GREAT CANDIDATE, BUT NOT QUALIFIED TO BE IN A RELATIONSHIP

---

2 WHY IS IT SO DIFFICULT FOR SINGLE GOOD MEN TO ABANDON SINGLEHOOD

---

3 THE SCREENING GUIDE: HOW NOT TO WASTE YOUR TIME

EPILOGUE

Preface

Knowledge Is the Equalizer

As you read this book keep an open mind and heart. I make generalizations about single men throughout the book, but remember that every man is unique in his own right. I did not write this book so that you can condemn, belittle or denigrate single men. I wrote it to empower you and to help you do a better job of selecting men who are truly qualified to be in relationships. As I thought about the pain that my nieces, aunts, cousins, sisters, female friends and clients have endured at the hands of single good men, I felt a strong need to provide you with information that will help you make healthier and more informed choices about the men who you allow to enter into your life.

On a regular basis, I am asked, "How do I deal with a single good man who is not truly interested in having a relationship?" My reply: "Acquire knowledge about single good men—our mind-set, behavior and mode of operation."

Without proper knowledge, your ability to understand and deal with single good men will not evolve. How often do you equip yourself with information that will help you solve or cope with the difficulties of interacting with single good men who do not commit? There are some things in life that you can excel in based on experimentation and practice; however, dealing with unpredictable single good men is not one of them.

Can you imagine what your life would be like if you secured personal and professional knowledge about men from the perspective of a man and combined it with your intuition?

Empower yourself by acquiring knowledge and applying it. *Remember that acquisition of knowledge is not power; application of knowledge is power*. Lack of understanding and knowledge is the root cause of most conflict between women and men. Do not continue to struggle unnecessarily. This book will enhance your ability to identify, screen and walk-away from qualified single good men who do not commit—remember that knowledge is the equalizer.

Yours Truthfully,

Dwayne L. Buckingham, Ph.D., LCSW, BCD

Introduction

Men Are Not Simple
Look Beyond the Surface

First things first—I would like to thank Steve Harvey for sharing his perspective about men with millions of women from different parts of the world. However, before I go further, I would like to remind you that Steve Harvey is a comedian, not a professional or licensed relationship expert. This is not a personal jab or attack against Steve Harvey. Personally, I like him as a comedian and outspoken man and feel that he should be praised for igniting a meaningful dialogue among millions of women around the world. His *personal views* and thoughts regarding the way men think and act have sparked a flame in women. He used humor and real life stories to drive his message home and left a lasting impression on young and old women who read, "*Act Like a Lady, Think Like a Man*" and "*Straight Talk, No Chaser*." Steve Harvey's personal view about men and relationships has prompted thousands of women to question men in a more serious manner. And I am one of those men.

While recently hanging out at a social event on Friday evening with some friends, I met this attractive young lady named Tina. After conversing with Tina for about twenty minutes, I asked if she would join me for dinner and "light" conversation on Sunday evening. She agreed, we exchanged phone numbers and returned to our associates. I enjoyed the rest of the evening and left the social event feeling psyched. I was excited and could not stop thinking about how attractive Tina looked. I was hoping that she was just as intelligent and down to earth as she was good looking.

Sunday arrived and per Tina's request, I picked her up from the metro station around 4 p.m. and we drove to a nice restaurant to have dinner and enjoy each other's company. As we dined, the questions began to flow in: Why are you still single? Do you want to be in a serious relationship? Are you trying to find out who you are? Are you still working to build your empire so you can take care of your future wife and children? Do you need to make more money? What drives you?

I hesitated before I answered the questions and asked myself, "Am I being screened with questions from Steve Harvey's books?" As I gathered my thoughts and composure I responded, "Yes, I am driven by who I am, what I do, and how much money I make; however none of those things personally influence my decision to remain single. I am comfortable with my identity as a single man and psychotherapist and thank God for blessing me with the ability to help people cope with and resolve their hardships. As an entrepreneur, I am blessed to be financially stable and take great pride in giving to individuals who are less fortune or in need. Overall, I am comfortable with my lifestyle as a single man."

After I finished sharing my thoughts, Tina looked me straight in my eyes and said, "You are not being honest. Don't lie to me. *All men are simple.* If none of those things influence your decision to remain single, then what does?" After being accused of being simple and a liar, I felt slightly disrespected. I also felt my blood pressure rising because I was being interrogated. As I set across the table from Tina, my mind drifted and I thought, "Steve Harvey obviously did not inform women about how to have timely and tactful conversations. I also thought that I should look Tina straight in her eyes, just like Jack Nicholson looked at Tom Cruise in the movie A Few Good Men, and say, "*You can't handle the truth!*"

Despite how I felt and what I thought, I decided to be respectful and to enlighten Tina. My response went as such, "I am not sure why you feel that I am lying to you. A large percentage of men, especially Black men do struggle with the issues Steve Harvey identified; however, my story is not the same as Steve Harvey's story or any other man's story. While it is true that most men engage in similar behavior, I do not believe that our behavior can be fully understood from the theoretical opinion of one man. There are many theories that attempt to explore why men struggle with relationships and Steve Harvey simply shared his theory. I have my own thoughts about men and relationships and so do other men. As a licensed and experienced psychotherapist, my thoughts regarding men and our behavior go beyond the surface views most men and women discuss on radio shows and in barber and beauty shops throughout America. I say this not to offend anyone or to minimize their opinions, but to basically emphasize that human behavior and development is a very complicated topic. Personal views, including mine, should be taken with a grain of salt. I encourage women to study and do their own research about men."

Tina replied, "I agree that this topic is very complicated. I continue to talk to men from different walks of life and still have not figured men out. So what are your thoughts Mr. Psychotherapist? Can you help me understand why single men, especially the good ones, do not commit? What's wrong with men like you?"

I hesitated again. This time I thought, "Is this the time and place to answer these questions?" After quickly playing through my mind how Tina might react again, I politely said, "I will share my thoughts with you another time." Tina, look puzzled, but said, "Okay." We finished dinner and I drove Tina back to the metro station and thanked her for having dinner with me.

After I dropped Tina off, I realized that I was slightly offended with her line of questioning and comment that, "*All men are simple.*" As I thought about our discussion, I realized that Tina was searching for understanding and clearly did not get all of her questions answered from reading Steve Harvey's books. I processed some more and came to the conclusion that men, including myself, are a little more complex than what is discussed on radio shows and in chat rooms.

Men are like gold. We shine on the outside, but in our rawest form, we are usually dull. I use this parallel to say that men are too complex to be taken for surface value. With this in mind, I decided to do as Steve Harvey did—enlighten you about men. However, unlike Steve Harvey, who informed you about men's secrets, I will inform you about the emotional and psychological issues behind the secrets that influence why good men remain single.

Have you ever asked yourself the following questions: "What makes single good men desirable? What makes men qualified for relationships? What emotional or psychological issues influence their decision to remain single? Why is it so difficult for good men to abandon singlehood? How can I identify and walk away from qualified men who will not commit?

Like most women, you have searched far and long for answers to the above-mentioned questions. Your search for answers has expanded your knowledge about men, but has also caused some frustration. I understand your frustration, but encourage you to continue your search for answers. I have three degrees in human behavior and development and have provided marital therapy to over twenty thousand women and men for the past fourteen years; and I, like you, still get frustrated with the whole woman and man relationship thing.

Understanding how men think, feel and act in relationships is not an easy task—there are a multitude of theories and explanations that attempt to provide insight into this phenomenon. I encourage you to study, but remember that there is no one "right" theory or explanation, so use what works for you and let the rest go. I do not claim to have all the answers in regards to men's thoughts or behavior, but I can tell you that men are not simple. If that was the case, this book and other relationship books would not exist.

Most women, especially single good women like yourself have been taught to select men who possess qualities that are compatible to yours. While this is good advice, have you ever thought about why so many single good men attract and subdue women without committing? Have you ever stopped to think about what most single good men have in common that makes them desirable? Please allow me to enlighten you.

We live in a society that places a great deal of emphasis on outwardly appearances, titles and status. Unfortunately, many of us take things at face value. I am guilty of this as well, but as a result of interacting with thousands of women and men with various life problems, *I have learned that behind every behavior there is an emotional or psychological issue associated with it.* For example, men who are focused on succeeding and work extremely hard could potentially be suffering from low self-esteem or insecurity. They may work hard because they feel that they have to prove themselves to others. Many people would say that there is nothing wrong with working hard—some men just have good work ethics. Sounds simple, right? I am not implying that all men who work hard are "screwed up or suffer from low self-esteem," but whatever their reasons are for working hard there are emotions associated with them. This is difficult for most women to identify and understand because most of you do not think to ask or don't care enough to explore the cause of men's behavior, especially if the behavior is good in nature. If a man possesses good qualities or attributes and is desirable, some of you might say, "Who cares if he works hard because he has low self-esteem or feels insecure as long as he brings the money home?"

For the women who care: What would you do if you met a man who was financially stable, presented well and treated you like a queen, but would not commit to you? This is a difficult question that many of you struggle with on a daily basis and the answer is not simple because there are plenty of men who shine on the outside, but struggle emotionally or psychologically. I know a lot of good men who are attractive, competent, reliable, genuine, enjoyable, kind, ambitious, successful and honorable, but will not commit to a woman. I socialize with men who attract women simply based on how they look. However, there are other men I socialize with who take care of business. Their A-Game is tight when it comes to taking care of their personal responsibilities and progressing professionally as single men. And before they approach you, they make sure that you cannot identify their emotional or psychological shortcomings too easily. Hiding their emotional shortcomings from you is not difficult because many of you do not know what to look for anyway. Some of you might wonder and ask yourself, "What's wrong with this man?", but will not follow through with your curiosity because you are impressed with his physical and/or intellectual presentation.

By now, I hope you understand why you have to look beyond the surface. Single good men are difficult to understand—some of us are willing to love and commit to you, but may struggle with unresolved emotional or psychological issues. Before single good men can give you what you desire (commitment), they must first resolve their own emotional or psychological issues. And since you are not equipped or skilled enough to recognize our emotional shortcomings, I have taken it upon myself to be your personal psychotherapist.

Qualified, yet Single is dedicated to all the single women like Tina, who desperately desire to understand why single men, especially the good ones, do not commit. This book is also dedicated to single good men who struggle to understand why they do not make that ultimate commitment.

As a result of going on many failed dates, I now realize that I, like you, have been influenced by all the wrong things when choosing a person to date. As previously stated, I think Steve Harvey did an excellent job with igniting a dialogue about men. And to add to your knowledge base, *Qualified, yet Single* will help you dig a little deeper—beyond men's surface or outwardly appearance.

In its most fundamental sense, *Qualified, yet Single* is a screening guide for women who are tired of wasting their time on single good men who struggle with commitment. Men's emotional problems should not be your responsibility to fix—demand that they resolve their own emotional shortcomings with or without you. No more excuses. This book offers a wealth of information that is based on seventeen plus years of personal experience as a single man, fourteen plus years of clinical experiences, and nine years of advanced academic instruction. If you are enticed or deceived by single good men who are not ready to commit, don't blame them. I hope that this book inspires you to think more deeply about men and to realize that behind every behavior there is an emotion.

Remember: *Qualified, yet Single* is your reminder that "All that glitters is not gold."

Part One

Great Candidate, But Not Qualified to Be in a Relationship

Chapter 1

Three Emotions that Enslave Single Good Men

Fear, Fixation and Firmness

One of the most challenging aspects of entering and sustaining a committed relationship with a man is your ability to identify and walk away from single good men who are great candidates but are not qualified to be in relationships. As you improve your screening skills and learn to look beyond a man's surface, you will understand that most single good men have the desire to settle down with the women of their dreams, buy the big white house in the suburbs and contribute to the birth of one and a half kids. However, a large percentage of us do not make that ultimate step toward oneness with that special woman because we are enslaved by fear, fixation and firmness. These three emotions typically dominate single good men and often dictate how we behave. If you do not learn anything else about single good men from this book, understand that fear, fixation and firmness are emotions that are deeply embedded in our psyche and often prevents many of us from entering into committed relationships and marrying. Stop wasting your time listening to men run "game" and start paying attention to our emotional makeup.

No matter how qualified a man may be—he will not commit to you or any other woman until he has successfully conquered his fear, eliminated his fixation and minimized his firmness. The more fear that a man experiences, the more fixated he will become, and his increased fixation will contribute to intense firmness. I refer to this as the Fear-Fixation-Firmness Cycle. And guess what? You are the trigger that sets this cycle in motion. Let me enlighten you about this emotionally debilitating cycle that enslaves most single good men.

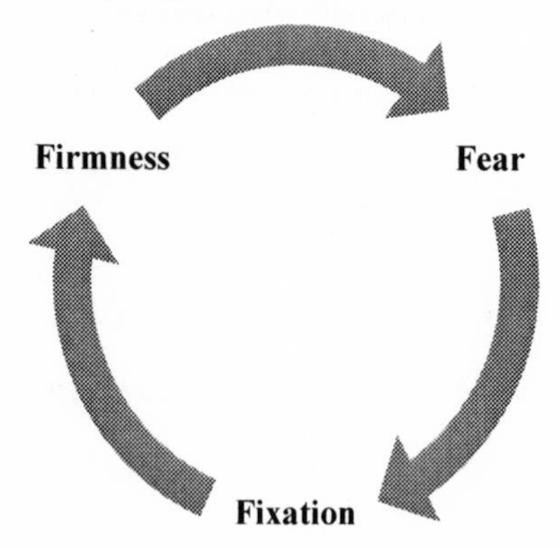

Fear

Fear is a distressing emotion that manifests psychologically when a man perceives that his well-being, identity, emotional stability or freedom is being or will be threatened. The loss of control or the threat of pain is often associated with fear. You may hear men say that they do not enter committed relationships because they are afraid of having one sex partner for the rest of their lives, afraid of losing their freedom or are afraid of being taken advantage of. While all of these things do create fear in men, I personally believe that the fear of falling in love or being emotionally vulnerable is what truly inhibits single good men from committing.

Falling in love or being emotionally vulnerable creates anxiety for men because it is associated with losing control, feeling weak and experiencing pain. In general, vulnerability is perceived to be very negative by most men. After years of reflecting on my relationship patterns, I realized that I would always find reasons to discredit and chase good women away because of my fear. Whenever I would start developing feelings for a woman I would experience this intense form of anxiety which often demobilized me. And the more I experienced fear, the more I pushed women away.

In the midst of my anxiety-provoking crisis years, I had difficulty entering and sustaining relationships with women without attempting to establish some emotional controls and boundaries. When dating, I made sure that women knew that I was not going to take them seriously. Looking back on my behavior, I now understand that I detached from women because I feared being vulnerable. The thought of being vulnerable and allowing myself to potentially be hurt by a woman, typically intensified my fear. If I experienced any distress or felt fearful as a result of something a woman said or did, I moved quickly to protect myself—I cut her off.

For many years, I did not understand why I reacted so strongly whenever I felt fearful, thought about losing control or being emotionally vulnerable. Year after year, I would find myself engaging in the same defensive behavior and would do whatever was needed to keep women at a distance. I realized that this behavior was not healthy for me, but I was in control of my emotions.

There were times during my mid-twenties when I longed for and desperately wanted to love and be loved by that special woman, but my fear would not allow me to lower my guards or remove my emotional armor. The desire to have companionship consumed me daily, but fear of being hurt and vulnerable had more of an emotional hold on me. Despite any efforts I made to accommodate or cater to women, I knew in my heart that I would not allow a woman to enter into my life until I understood and conquered my fear.

The pursuit of understanding and conquering my fear was not an easy task. How often do you hear men talk about their fear? Probably not too often because we typically do not discuss our emotions, especially emotions that make us look weak. It is not cool to be viewed as being weak when interacting with women so most of us do not disclose how we truly feel. We have been taught that men should not show fear or vulnerability. Fear is perceived by the majority of men, especially Black men, as some minor emotion that should be ignored or met with aggression. Given this stereotypical mindset, I would not disclose my fear or if I did share, I felt that women did not connect with me because they perceived me as being either too arrogant or aggressive.

Date after date, I found myself feeling empty as I struggled with the fact that I could enjoy women's physical company, but would not allow myself to give in or connect with them emotionally. As with most men, I suppressed how I really felt and began my journey towards understanding and conquering my fear in solitude and silence. Attempting to understand the source of my fear consumed me emotionally for many years.

Then, one night while laying in bed I began to think deeply about all of my past relationships and processed how each one impacted my behavior and perceptions of women. After playing each relationship over and over in my head, there was one that stood out and caused me to feel anxious instantly. I'll never forget the fear, pain and vulnerability that I experienced after going through a difficult and upsetting break-up while in college. Reflecting on my college dating experience helped me understand the source of my fear.

During my sophomore year in college, I met this attractive young lady name Monica who was enrolled in one of my psychology classes. Initially, I had no intentions of dating or being serious with Monica because she was nine months pregnant. But as we interacted, I felt some emotional and physical chemistry develop, so I inquired about her situation and relationship status. Monica informed me that she had gotten pregnant by a guy she dated for a short period, but was no longer with him because he left her after getting her pregnant. I did not think much about her situation; after all I was not looking to start a serious relationship.

Monica was a southwestern girl who had a good spirit and always appeared to be happy despite her situation. Her positive spirit was intoxicating so I began to flirt with her and we decided to hang out. Shortly, after we started hanging out, Monica delivered her daughter, Jessica. At first, I was not too concerned about being involved with a young female who had just delivered a child, because my "other head" was dictating most of my decisions and moves at that point in my life.

After Monica gave birth to Jessica, our interactions increased and I began to look forward to hanging-out with her during the weekends at her mother's house. The very first day that I visited, Monica's ex-boyfriend called and threatened to come over because she told him that she had company. Monica mentioned this to me, but I was not concerned because I did not know the guy, plus he never showed up.

In the coming months Monica and I spent a great deal of time together so she decided to get her own apartment. I spent nights at her place and we enjoyed each others' company. I was skating on cloud nine and thought I was doing it "big" because I had a female who had her own place and was willing to feed and sex me anytime.

During the earlier stage of the relationship, Monica would take her daughter to her mother's house so that her ex-boyfriend could pick her up from there. This was fine with me because I did not feel a need to meet the guy, especially since I thought he was a bum for leaving his woman while she was pregnant. We never talked about her ex-boyfriend, so I did not know much about him. Monica did not feel a need to tell me anything about him and I did not feel a need to ask. I guess we were in love and did not want to say or do anything that would damage our relationship. At that point in my life, I did not know what love meant, but I felt something close it. We were living a peaceful fairytale relationship.

Monica and I kicked it for approximately nine months before our fairytale relationship changed. As time passed, she got tired of dropping her daughter off at her mother's house, so she decided to tell her ex-boyfriend where she lived so he could pick their daughter up from the apartment. This single decision significantly impacted our relationship and we never recovered.

July 12, 1994 was the day I learned what it feels like to experience the loss of control in a relationship. I also learned about the pain that is associated with being emotionally vulnerable. On this particular day, Monica's ex-boyfriend showed up to pick up their daughter. As he entered the apartment around 4:30 p.m., I was sitting on the couch watching football. He introduced himself and asked who was playing. I introduced myself and mentioned the names of the two football teams. He gathered Jessica's belongings and left with her. Shortly after he left, the phone rang and I heard Monica raise her voice. Within 30 minutes of the phone call, her ex-boyfriend returned and dropped Jessica back off.

I inquired about what was going on and Monica told me that her ex-boyfriend was mad because she had another man around his daughter. I asked if I needed to leave and Monica said, "No, everything is okay." We went on with our day and got in bed around midnight. At approximately 2 a.m. in the morning, I was woken by kicking and loud knocking at the front door. Monica jumped out of bed and rushed to the door because she did not want the noise to wake up Jessica. I could hear Monica's ex-boyfriend say, "Let me in to see my damn daughter. I am going back to California in the morning and I want to see my damn daughter." After he finished yelling and cursing, I heard Monica say, "You have been drinking. Leave or I will call the police." At this point, I decided to get out of the bed so that I could check on Monica. As I rolled out of bed, I heard Monica say, "Don't push me," and then I heard the door hit the wall. I quickly put on my shorts and attempted to stand up, but before I could stand-up completely, Monica's ex-boyfriend grabbed me. We tossed and turned until we ended up in the living room. He attempted to hit me and I attempted to hit him.

Monica was crying and screaming, "You better leave my apartment now or I will call the police." She ran to the bedroom and grabbed her gun and the telephone. By the time she entered the living room, we had stopped wrestling. Monica told her ex-boyfriend to leave, but he refused. She handed me the gun and called the police.

The police arrived and asked me if I wanted to press charges for assault and battery. I told the police that I didn't want to press charges because I felt that I could address the issue without getting the judicial system involved. The police encouraged me to file a report in case something bad happened in the future. With a hostile look on my face, I replied, "I can take care of it myself. I am not worried about having anything on file." They took the hand-cuffs off Monica's ex-boyfriend and allowed him to leave.

To make a long story short, I spent the next few months on an emotionally roller coaster. Monica's ex-boyfriend threatened me often and occasionally showed up at my job. And as a result I started carrying a gun to work daily and eventually decided to quit my job because I did not want anything to happen to innocent people.

In an attempt to support me and protect herself, Monica got a restraining order against her ex-boyfriend. I was glad that Monica was looking out for me, but the drama was taking a toll on me emotionally. Nevertheless, I decided to hang in there with Monica for a few more months because I felt like I was in love. The love thing was new to me so I did not know how to deal with pain that sometimes accompanies love. I did not know that loving someone could be so dramatic and painful. This was all new to me and I had never felt so vulnerable and out of control before.

After having frequent intense encounters with Monica's ex-boyfriend, I decided to call it a quits. I told Monica that I felt that it would be best for everyone if I just moved on with my life. She was devastated, but understood. We both felt hurt and defeated. Walking away was emotionally devastating for me, but I knew that I could not remain in the relationship any longer. We decided to remain friends and I told Monica that I would check on her from time to time.

Several weeks passed before I decided to call to check on Monica. I had mixed feelings about calling because I still had strong feelings for her. Nevertheless, I decided to call one Saturday morning to check on her. When she answered the phone she appeared to be distant and short with me. I was somewhat bothered and hurt because that was not Monica's normal way of acting. Confused and concerned, I decided to stop by her apartment. When she answered the door and saw me, her faced dropped. Monica looked like she had just seen a ghost. I asked her what was wrong and she said she did not want any trouble. As I entered the apartment, I saw her daughter crawling by the bedroom door. I immediately, thought, "Why is the baby in the back of the apartment alone?"

I began to walk down the hall and Monica shouted, "I don't want any trouble." As I opened the door her ex-boyfriend was laying across the bed with no clothes on. My heart dropped immediately and I thought, "I should attack his ass, like he attacked me." But despite how I felt, I decided to leave. I left the apartment immediately and drove around for approximately 30 minutes to gather myself. I was not in a good place emotionally. One side of my mind was telling me to go back to the apartment and shoot his ass and the other side of mind was telling me to let it go.

Disturbed and confused, I returned to the apartment with a gun in my pocket. I knocked on the door and told Monica that I wanted to talk to her and her ex-boyfriend. She begged me not to start any trouble if she allowed me to come in. I promised not to start any trouble so she opened the door. As she opened the door she started crying and apologizing. She could see the hurt and pain in my eyes. I did not say anything to her. I approached her ex-boyfriend and sat across from him on the couch. I stared at him with my hand in my pocket. He was not sure how to respond to me because he could see the anger in my eyes, plus he did not know what was in my pocket.

I took a deep breath and started talking. I told him that he better do right by Monica because he put me through so much shit just to get her back. He looked at me and said, "I know she is a good woman and I plan to do right this time." I asked him to leave the living room so that Monica and I could talk alone. I asked Monica why she decided to get back with her ex-boyfriend after all the drama he had put us through. Monica replied, "I did not feel that any other man would deal with the drama that you dealt with. Also, I felt trapped because he is father of my daughter." I understood what Monica was saying on an intellectual level, but I was still filled with hurt and anger. I walked out of Monica's apartment that day in pain and feeling very vulnerable. *As I drove out of the apartment complex, I vouched that I would never allow myself to feel that way again.* I never spoke to Monica again, but heard that she had eventually married her ex-boyfriend.

With a multitude of women on campus, I quickly put the experience behind me and started hanging out with other young women. I spent my last year in college having sex with a few different women and kicking it with my fraternity brothers. I told females up-front that I was only interested in having sex and fun. Women accepted my position and my remaining days in college were fulfilled by attending fraternity parties and having sex with a multitude of young women who were not interested in having a serious relationship.

The emotional, "I want to be in-love" young man had disappeared and so did my desire to be in a committed relationship. I finished undergraduate and enrolled in graduate school at Michigan State University a year later. I started a new chapter in my life, but my perception about committed relationships and interaction with women did not change.

The reason I share my story is to help you understand that *behind every behavior there is an emotion.* Please understand that men do not act up without having a reason. Some men may lack insight and give simple reasons for their behavior, but believe me whatever their reason is for their behavior, there is an underlying emotion associated with it. I am here to tell you that educated, successful, confident, ambitious and highly-respected men are typically the ones who have the most difficulty with understanding and conquering our fear. I say this because my fear intensified as I achieved success. I did not feel comfortable discussing or sharing my fear with women who perceived me to be the "total" package. Women frequently placed me on a pedestal and often asked, "Why are you still single?" Like most single good men, I usually responded by saying, "I can't find a good woman, I am focusing on my career, I am finishing school or I am too picky." But deep down inside I wanted to say, "I am scared as hell."

For a long time I did not disclose my fear to anyone, especially women, because most women were more impressed with the initials behind my name. They did not truly care to understand my emotional temperament. So, despite my underlying fear and unwillingness to commit, I did not have a problem attracting women and keeping them within hands reach just in case I felt a need to be entertained or pleasured sexually. To be truthful, keeping women within hands reach for pleasure and entertainment purposes became much easier as I enhanced my money making potential.

Similar to most single, successful and ambitious men, I quickly learned that a large percentage of women would tolerate nonsense and wait around for a man who is perceived to be a great candidate, especially if he has a decent financial portfolio and presents well. As I dated, I realized that my charming, considerate and respectful qualities along with my financial stability placed me in a position to dictate the nature and frequency of my interactions with women. Some women liked the fact that I was stern and confident, so I got away with dealing with them on my terms.

Most single good men understand that women are impressed by men who present as being strong and fearless, so it is not difficult to convince them to fall into place. If a man can manipulate and dominate a woman while masking his fear, he will do exactly that. We will typically do whatever is needed to avoid being hurt or feeling too vulnerable.

Understand that fear is an anxiety-provoking emotion that drives single good men into self-preservation mode. Pay attention to our reactions when we feel threatened. You will notice that most of us say or do things that are intended to protect and preserve ourselves. And although this self-preservation behavior is natural for men and women who feel fearful, men often do not address their fear head on, especially in relationships.

No matter how confident a man may appear on the outside, he will not be able to offer you emotional security, love or commitment if he has not conquered his fear. In fact, unconquered fear will cause him to suffer from fixation and will definitely keep the *Fear-Fixation-Firmness Cycle* in full rotation.

Fixation

Fixation has to do with a man's state of mind and is best defined as an unhealthy and compulsive preoccupation with something or someone. The most debilitating component of fixation is obsession, which refers to a fixed idea or unwanted emotion that is associated with fear. You probably know men who have one-track minds. Their minds are completely obsessed with a single thought or idea and they rarely entertain alternative viewpoints.

Men who experience fixation typically express it through their stories. For example, whenever a woman inquired about my past relationships, I always mentioned the relationship that I had during my sophomore year in college. It never failed; time after time I shared that experience with every woman who asked me about my previous relationships. The more I thought about it, the more I realized that that single relationship played a major factor in how I interacted with and treated women. The loss of control and vulnerability that I felt during my college puppy love experience was deeply embedded in my psyche. I played that painful experience over and over in mind as I ventured into manhood and began to date other women. This is what fixation truly means. My mind was often preoccupied with that experience and no matter how much I cared about a woman, I always thought about the hurt and pain I endured while dating in college. That experience caused me to become obsessed with avoiding painful and vulnerable emotions. My fixation with pain and not feeling vulnerable led to an emotional coldness that surfaced when women attempted to strip me of my emotional armor.

When a man is in full fixation mode, his inflexibility and firmness will kick in order to prevent you from breaking down or stripping him of his emotional armor. Just think about it: if you were afraid of something or did not have adequate skills to cope, you would likely rely on skills you developed from previous experiences to protect yourself. This is what men do. We fixate and then become firm because we are afraid. Unresolved fixation will keep the Fear-Fixation-Firmness cycle in rotation because most men will become inflexible and firm—"no means no." Firmness is displayed in order to prevent potentially painful or vulnerable experiences from re-occurring.

Firmness

The ability to control and safeguard one's emotions in relationships drives most single good men. And anything or anybody that poses a threat will be met with resistance or hostility. Firmness is an emotional reaction that often surfaces in men when thoughts of pain arise. Once a man perceives that he will lose control, his firmness or unwillingness to compromise will intensify. And he will say and do whatever is needed to maintain control of the situation. Unfortunately, as his fear intensifies, so will his firmness.

You have probably noticed that a lot of men struggle with compromising, especially if they perceive that they will be left feeling vulnerable. Demonstrating firmness is our way of saying,

"I'm in control." During this period, you will not be able to reason with us because we are most likely feeding off of fear. When fear is present or perceived, our reactions are more instinctive in nature—protect or destroy. Verbal attacks, stubbornness or irrational behavior will likely occur when we are locked into "firm" man mode. Firmness is a coping or adaptability technique that we use to safeguard ourselves and to prevent fear and pain from impacting and dominating us. Men will show firmness in many ways. For me, firmness was illustrated through my unwillingness to date women with children. From my heartbreaking college experience, I learned that some women who have baby daddies are not in positions to freely negotiation how they want to live their lives. As long as their baby's father is involved or paying child support, he will always have the right to be a part of his child's life, and in some ways he can also impact the child's mother. With this in mind, I became adamant about not dating women with children. And although I realized that Monica's boyfriend was crazy, my fear and fixation regarding the experience basically intensified my firmness.

See ladies, this is what unconquered fear does to a number of men, even single good men. It sets unreasonable thinking into play and some of us become very firm in our thinking and doing, even if it is irrational. Sometimes we will argue and even start fights just to show you that we have the ability to control or dominate situations. Sounds terrible and immature, right? It is, but men will frequently respond in a firm manner whenever we are upset or afraid. Many of us have not been taught to express ourselves assertively and putting our foot down occasionally is a rite of passage that every man believes that he has earned. I personally believe that it is okay to be firm, but men who respond in a firm manner out of fear, should be called on the carpet.

Men are not very courageous when it comes to addressing and dealing with emotions, especially fear. Most of us are scared as hell. Emotions do not have a reasoning component associated with them; therefore men struggle with understanding the feeling aspect of relationships. With time and support, some of us can and do learn to conquer our fear, reduce our fixation and minimize our firmness. However, I must warn you that breaking the Fear-Fixation-Firmness Cycle is not an easy process for most men. We operate from a mind over matter perspective, which means we reason first and then feel.

Take Home Message

As you explore your options on the dating scene, remember that some single good men are great candidates, but those who have not conquered their fear will most likely not be qualified for the job—entering and sustaining a committed relationship with you.

5 Common Types of Fears Single Men Experience

Below is a list of the common types of fears that influence men's decisions to remain single and avoid commitment.

1. Fear of Abandonment—occurs when a man is afraid that women will eventually leave them or walk out of their lives. Men in this category will take drastic means to hold on to intimate companionship or avoid it at all cost.

2. Fear of Losing Peer Support and Approval—men suffer this fear because they do not like to be referred to as a sell-out and ultimately lose their peer support. Men in this category dread the idea of changing their lifestyle because they will be viewed differently by their peers. Peer acceptance is important to them.

3. Fear of Changing Lifestyle—Men in this category dread comprising and adjustment, and they struggle with the idea that they will have to change their lives and be more open to having another person in their life.

4. Fear of Being Emotionally Vulnerable—some men are afraid to share and express emotions out of fear of being hurt. Men in this category typically do not trust women with their emotions or feelings.

5. Fear of Losing Their Freedom—the idea of giving up their independence is anxiety provoking. Men in this category fear that they will be restricted and limited if they commit. They can't sleep who they want to sleep with, go where they want to go or buy what they want to buy.

Chapter 2

Men Are Skilled in Psychological Warfare, Not Emotional Warfare: Emotions–What Are Those?

"I want to be close to you, but not emotionally. I have been thinking about my future and I want to keep my options open. I like you and want to keep our thing going, but I want you to know that I am not ready for a serious relationship. I am saying this because I care about you and do not want to hurt your feelings. I'm just being honest with you."

How many times have you heard a man say this to you or one of your girls? Every man in the world has spoken the aforementioned words at some point in his life. By now, you have probably learned that men are skilled and well prepared to engage in psychological warfare. Some of the things that come out of our mouths make good sense from an intellectual standpoint, but often lack emotional sensitivity. This happens because from the time we are little boys, we receive extensive psychological warfare training, but no emotional warfare training. Let me clarify what I mean.

The average little boy is instructed to "use his head" and to think on an average of forty times a week. When little boys injure themselves, behave inappropriately or make bad decisions, they are quickly reminded of what they should have done differently. They are encouraged to *think*, but are rarely given any guidance about how they should *feel*. And unfortunately, this one-sided instructional process that focuses on nurturing the intellect continues as little boys transition into teens and young men.

Some men hear the words, "Do you ever think?" on an average of sixty times a week. After years of being instructed to think, little boys become men who have crafted the ability to successfully engage in psychological warfare. And before we present something to you, believe me, we have thought about it. We might not always come up with the best solution or sound intelligent, but we often think before we respond. The problem that most women have with men is centered on the fact that we often lack emotional sensitivity, not intellectual aptitude. Simply stated: Learning how to identify and address emotions is challenging for men because we operate in different reasoning spheres than you.

Most of you would agree that men primarily operate from an intellectual sphere and women primarily operate from an emotional sphere. Men are often driven by intellect and believe that facts are as equally important or more important than emotions. Objectivity or impartiality plays a vital role in how men make decisions in relationships. Men typically do not express sensitive or nurturing emotions without apprehension and pre-calculating the risk. Women are the other hand, are often driven by emotions and believe that feelings are as equally important or more important than facts. Subjectivity or emotionality plays a vital role in how most of you make decisions in relationships.

The difference in intellectual and emotional aptitude between women and men is what leads to all out warfare. Men typically display very high intellectual aptitudes in relationships. In comparison, women typically display very high emotional aptitudes. For example, men speak and behave based on how we think. Our emotional capacity is not necessarily inadequate, but is regularly dominated by our intellect. In contrast, you speak and behave based on how you feel. Your intellectual capacity is not necessarily inadequate, but is commonly dominated by your emotions. Men use intellect to guard our hearts from emotional pain. We rely heavily on our intellect to cope with, understand and process relationships and life challenges. When we are forced to deal with emotions, we are likely to become frustrated if our intellect fails us. Our desire to rationalize everything typically prevents us from feeling wholeheartedly and subjectively.

Personally, I believe that it is unfortunate that men have become so skilled in the art of psychological warfare. Through socialization, we have learned to rationalize inappropriate behavior, suppress our emotions and engage in tactical warfare in our relationships. We use various intellectual techniques to influence your values, beliefs, emotions and behavior and our ultimate goal is to induce you to do what we want you to do. Through the art of psychological warfare we have learned to manipulate women. This sounds disturbing, right? As I thought about this behavior and surveyed hundreds of men, I found that men engage in psychological warfare, not with the intent to hurt women, but in order to position themselves to be in control as they enter into in relationships.

Too often men will decide to causally hang-out with you and demand that you provide all the benefits associated with being in a relationship, but refuse to invest emotionally in you or the relationship. Some men search for ways to take advantage of people and situations in every aspect of our lives, including business ventures and relationships. Scoring what we want in relationships without fighting the fight is the primary purpose of engaging in psychological warfare. We are groomed to be conquerors and to take pride in being able to prevent people, especially women, from scamming and hurting us.

As men, we have definitely learned how to get our "ice-cream" and "cake" by engaging in psychological warfare with you. To illustrate how men are skilled at engaging in psychological warfare, let's revisit and dissect the quote I listed at the beginning of this chapter:

> I want to be close to you, but not emotionally. I have been thinking about my future and I want to keep my options open. I like you and want to keep our thing going, but I want you to know that I am not ready to be serious. I am saying this because I care about you and do not want to hurt your feelings. I'm just being honest.

As you read the quote above, what do you hear and feel? Are you capable of deciphering the message in the quote? This is a classic quote that thousands of men use daily because it communicates interest, foresight, hope, concern, genuineness and honesty. This particular technique is called subliminal persuasion and is designed to influence you emotionally. The ultimate goal is to keep you hanging on.

Men use subliminal persuasion to get what we want while also coming across as being charming. Our messages are very charming and crafted in a positive manner in order to prevent you from noticing the hidden messages. We want you to think highly of us while doing things that you might not want to do. This is psychological warfare at its best.

Breakdown 1: The Good Message

Sentence #1: He communicates interest—"*I want to be close to you.*" Sentence #2: He communicates foresight—"*I have been thinking about my future.*" Sentence #3: He communicates interest and hope—"*I like you and want to keep our thing going.*" Sentences #4 and #5: He communicates concern, genuineness and honesty—"*I am saying this because I care about you and do not want to hurt your feelings. I'm just being honest.*"

Breakdown 2: The Hidden Message

Sentence #1: He communicates that he does not want to be attached—"*but not emotionally.*" Sentence #2: He communicates that he wants his freedom—"*I want to keep my options open.*" Sentence #3: He communicates lack of interest—"*but I want you to know that I am not ready to be serious.*" Sentences #4 and #5: He communicates honesty to avoid hurting you—"*I do not want to hurt your feelings. I'm just being honest.*"

Some women lack the intellectual aptitude to dissect and understand hidden messages and others just choose to ignore them. This is your biggest mistake when dealing with men, especially good men. It is not easy to dissect the hidden messages of good guys because our tactics are different than bad guys. Good guys will express how we feel without sugar coating our thoughts, but will use positive and inspiring words so that you do not to pick up the hidden message. Bad guys on the other hand, will try to manipulate you, but will use negative and belittling words so that you clearly get the message. When a good man tells you that he is not emotionally available or interested in a serious relationship, he will be kind about doing so.

Men are capable of getting our "ice cream" and "cake" because you hear what you want to hear. I would advise you to stop allowing your emotions to control you and start using your God-given intellect. As mentioned previously, men are not as emotionally attuned as you are because most of us have not received proper training. Whether it is right or wrong, we will try to make you feel bad about falling for us because you did not recognize what was being told to you up front. Remember, most of us operate from an intellectual sphere, and when dealing with men who lack emotional aptitude or are emotionally unavailable, you are likely to experience condemnation for being too emotional.

There is nothing in the world that is more challenging and stressful for a woman than being in a relationship with or having a genuine interest in a man who is emotionally unavailable. Ninety percent of the women that I see for individual consultation and marital therapy struggle in their marriages because they are married to men who are emotionally unavailable.

Listen to me when I tell you that men who are emotionally unavailable can and will suck the life out of you and will not experience much distress while doing so. I make it sound as if men are evil and have no heart. This is not the case by far; some men just miss the mark when it comes to recognizing and responding to emotions, especially if they are not truly interested in you or are emotionally unavailable—"Emotions, what are those?"

Some men are emotionally unavailable because they have difficulty with recognizing emotions and others chose to be emotionally unavailable because they are consumed by career aspirations, school or work obligations, peer pressure, success, selfishness or heartache from a previous relationship.

Men who are emotionally unavailable do not invest heartfelt time and energy into women. Your chances of being hurt are greater during this period of emotional seclusion that some men venture off into; therefore it is imperative that you learn how to assess whether or not a man will be emotionally available to you (more on this in Chapter 10).

Emotionally unavailable men want what every man wants—your time, your body, your mind, your companionship and your undivided attention. He wants you to be there for him emotionally, physically and spiritually, but will not give the same in return. Most women do not get or understand this.

Here are a few stories that illustrate how women get hurt by men who are emotionally unavailable.

Story #1

Rob (age 33) and Janet (age 27) have been seeing each and other for approximately five months. When they first met, Rob told Janet that he was not interested in a having serious relationship, but wanted companionship. Janet agreed to Rob's terms and they began to hang out on a regular basis. Although Rob had no intentions of being with Janet seriously, he still went out of his way to treat her special. He bought her gifts, took her on trips and wined and dined her.

After several months of hanging out, Janet told Rob that she was starting to fall in love with him and would like to discuss the possibility of having a serious relationship. Rob looked Janet in her eyes and asked, "Why are you getting all emotional and changing up on me now?" Janet was somewhat stunned and replied, "I thought you really liked me because we spend a lot of time together and you treat me really well."

Rob replied, "I was very clear about my intentions from jump start. I treated you like a good man is supposed to treat a woman. It was not my intent to lead you on. What do you want me to do?"

Story #2

Trina (age 27) met John (age 29) while he was in his second year of law school. John was going through a lot and was having a hard time staying focused on school. He told Trina that he was interested in having a serious relationship and possibly getting married after law school, but was simply looking for noncommittal companionship for now because he does not want to lose focus.

Trina accepted John's terms. John took Trina around his friends and even took her home to meet his parents. John's parents liked Trina, but were concerned that John was being distracted by her. John reassures his parents that Trina is not a distraction because he has no plans of being in a serious relationship anytime in the near future.

Four months pass and Trina really starts to dig John. She asks, "Do you think there is a possibility of us being more serious with each other? I know you said that you do not want to lose focus while you are in school, but things have changed between us, right?"

John replies, "I like you a lot and things have changed, but I am not interested in being in a serious relationship. I am not ready or willing to dedicate the time that is required to be serious with you. I know I took you home with me to meet my parents, but I agreed to it because you wanted to go. I did not ask you to go."

Who's at fault? Are the men wrong for sticking to their original agreements? If a man tells you that he is emotionally unavailable, pay attention and keep it moving or prepare yourself to deal with the repercussions.

In every relationship, whether it is formal or informal, each individual is responsible for his or her emotions. If the man that you are with has difficulty recognizing and responding to your emotional needs, do not blame him if you stay with him. Learn to establish some boundaries and be firm about what you want and how you want to be treated. Do not expect an emotionally unavailable man to be responsible for or considerate of how you feel. You are responsible for how you feel. Understand that some men are not willing to take responsibility for their actions so it is up to you to protect your heart.

Under no circumstances should you allow a man to attack or demean you for showing or expressing emotions toward him. However, you cannot get mad or upset if he does not show or express the same emotions toward you. God gave women and men the gift of *free will* so that we could think, feel and behave however we want. Therefore, you need to stop trying to persuade men to do things that we do not want to do. You should express your concerns and needs and move on if you are not happy.

Do not play mind-games trying to think like men. You will never been able to think like us, nor should you want to. A man who is ready and wants to be committed has already done some preparation prior to you meeting you. If he has not taken adequate steps prior to meeting you, he probably will not, and if he does, his actions will probably be for all the wrong reasons—sex or ego tripping.

You know what you want and need emotionally. If a man is not capable of connecting with you emotionally, he should not be allowed to connect with you in any other manner, especially sexually. Healthy relationships are built on emotional intimacy, not physical or intellectual intimacy.

A man's high intellectual aptitude might draw you toward him, but his low emotional aptitude will definitely chase you away. Men who take pride in engaging in psychological warfare in their relationships can become your worst nightmare. Take-heed: when a man tells you that he is not emotionally available—he means just that.

Take Home Message

Some men might be great candidates from an intellectual stance, but without emotional sensitivity, availability and maturity they are not qualified to be in relationships.

Chapter 3

Four Relationship Qualities Single Good Men Lack

Some men have great qualities and present well in professional, social, familial and interpersonal situations. They shine when interacting with their mothers, sisters, nieces, aunts and female friends. You see this behavior and do not question their ability to enter into and sustain relationships. You never think to ask yourself, "How can men who are so gentle with and responsive to women, be single?" You are mesmerized by their mannerisms and wish that you could be a part of their lives.

Your intellectual blinders are shut tight and you do not want to open them to see clearly. Strong good woman like yourself like to be challenged so you convince yourself to believe that you can make any man fall in love with you, especially if you express a little nurturing and sex appeal.

Most of you are convinced that you have what it takes to change a man and believe that you can persuade a man to commit to you and treat you well if you give him enough sex, show him appreciation and submit. This distorted thinking on your behalf is why most of you have problems with entering into and sustaining healthy and lasting relationships. You fail to realize that your behavior is just a contribution and not the sole or primary factor that determines how men feel, think or behave.

Men are like microwave food. We are prepackaged and appear to be simple, but if you do not read and follow the instructions that are listed on the back of the package, you can screw things up and have a big mess on your hands. As a woman you can relate to the frustration that occurs when you have your heart and mind set on preparing your favorite dish, but as you begin to cook you realize that you do not have all of the proper ingredients. Your lack of preparation prevents you from getting what you desire. Well, as I interact with other single men in social and professional settings, I have come to learn that some of us desire to be in relationships, but do not commit or enter into relationships because we lack certain ingredients or qualities that are needed to do well in a relationship.

Every woman dreams of having a relationship with a man who is: 1) secure in his identity; 2) trusting of women; 3) emotionally resilient and 4) possess realistic expectations. From the beauty shops to nail shops across America, women express their distaste for men who are insecure, untrusting of women, emotionally rigid and possess unrealistic expectations. However, many of you end up dating and in some instances marrying men who lack the four basic relationship qualities mentioned above. If you what to determine if a man is capable of entering into and sustaining a relationship, you must familiarize yourself with the four basic relationship qualities that most single good men lack. Be mindful that some single good men may lack all four qualities, while others might only lack one or two. The number of qualities that a man lacks is not as important as the behavior that occurs as a result of his deficit.

Identity Security

Failure to develop and to sustain identity security is the first relationship quality that single men lack. In my opinion, identity security in a relationship is not all about a man's ability to accumulate material possessions, provide financial stability for his family and possesses certain titles. *Identity security is about conducting oneself like a REAL man by expressing sensitive emotions and demonstrating vulnerability.* A man who is secure in his identity has the ability to cope with doubt, anxiety and fear. He is not preoccupied with losing control by showing his woman that he cares—he does not pretend to be confident, he *is* confident.

The thought of losing control is unbearable for men. Therefore, we find security in titles and other insignificant things because we feel powerful and in control. We thrive when we are capable of protecting and providing for our family because we feel in control. We feel that we have earned the right and distinct honor of being called a real man if we put food on the table, keep our family members safe, possess respected titles and provide clothing and shelter. According to Steve Harvey, most men are driven by being able to perform and accomplish these things.

I agree, but I would argue that most men are missing the mark on a daily basis when it comes to truly understanding and embracing the role of being a REAL man.

In my guesstimate, thousands of men are misinformed about what it means to be a REAL man; therefore many of us have identity issues and struggle with feeling secure in our relationships. Right about now, you are probably asking yourself, "What makes a man a *REAL* man and what does that have to do with identity security?"

I am glad you asked.

If you pick up any relationship book, search the internet or read blogs about relationships and men, you will probably find numerous definitions about what it means to be a *REAL* man. For example, I have heard women say, "A REAL man gives up one night stands for a woman he can't stand to live without." I have also heard women say, "A REAL man doesn't play games with a woman's heart." And finally, I have heard women say, "A REAL man takes care of his home."

On a daily basis women and men are having conversations about this topic because there are many definitions and myths about what it means to be a real man. Most of the conversations that I hear about what a REAL man is and is not are centered on myths about men being macho.

I personally believe that all myths about men should be explored in some form or fashion, however, as a relationship expert, I would be remiss if I did not address the two myths that cause the most damage in relationships: "men are strong and don't show sensitive emotions" and "men are proud and do not apologize." As I debunk each myth, I will highlight how they negatively impact men's behavior and summarize the truths about each myth.

Myth 1: A *REAL* Man Is Strong and Does Not Cry or Show Sensitive Emotions!

It is not uncommon for you to hear men say, "A REAL man is strong and does not cry or show sensitive emotions." Men will typically engage in tough behavior in order to maintain our manhood. Acting feminine by giving freely or expressing sensitive or nurturing emotions is viewed as being unmanly. The pressure to maintain our masculinity and to remain strong often creates emotional roadblocks for us.

The negative impact: Men minimize and occasionally suppress sensitive emotions in order to maintain our masculinity. Often we become defensive and feel frustrated and angry when someone questions our masculinity. Increased emotional distress experienced by men often leads to a refusal to express sadness or pain in a sensitive or appropriate manner.

Words of affection are viewed as a sign of weakness and are expressed only in desperate situations, i.e. the end of a relationship, pending divorce or separation. This insensitive behavior contributes to the conflict experienced in many of our relationships. Instead of saying "I am sorry" or "I was wrong," many of us will allow our relationships to end and even abandon our families.

Many of us have a desire to express sensitive emotions and demonstrate compassion, but lack the ability to because we were not trained properly. Our perception of manhood and what it means to be a REAL man is built on false beliefs.

Our primary drive as men is to feel safe and secure. We live, eat and breathe to prove that we are secure in our identities and are capable of dealing with whatever comes our way.

Whether a man is rich or poor, educated or uneducated, his primary goal in life, generally speaking, is to be a conqueror and to be in control. Money, titles and positions are things that we chase after because we feel that we are REAL men once we have acquired them. However, the acquisition of these things does not make a REAL man.

Men are groomed into believing that the possession of money and titles is what determines manhood. This belief system is what has most of us walking around with self-esteem issues and feeling depressed, unhappy and insecure if we do not have these things. And a large percentage of us believe that we should not commit to you unless we are balling out of control and can take care of your every need. This is unfortunate because men who acquire material things and titles typically believe we are REAL men because we are capable of providing for and protecting women and children.

The truth: A REAL man is a great provider and protector, but he does not limit his ability to express the God-given emotions he was blessed with. A REAL man will learn to acknowledge and express sensitive emotions in his relationship because he realizes that he gets what he gives. A REAL man eliminates the “tough guy, I don’t care” persona because he understands that it will only distance himself from you—the woman he loves. A REAL man does not allow this male dominant society to prevent him from sharing his gift of compassion with you. A REAL man is okay with showing affection toward you because he understands that he needs a good balance of emotional expression in order to have a healthy relationship.

A REAL man does not worry about what other men think about him and will express affection for you when he feels it. A REAL man understands that the expression of sensitive emotions does not convey that he is weak or feminine; it does convey that he is compassionate. A REAL man understands that God created humans, both men and women, with a full range of emotions because He understood that men, like women, could not appreciate happiness without sadness, calmness without anger, laughter without crying, empathy without judgment, and love without hate. A REAL man understands that expressing sensitive emotions is natural and doing so will enable to him share what's in his heart.

Take Home Message

A REAL man is confident, secure in his identity and does not have a problem with opening up to the woman in his life, particularly if it will bring peace into his home and relationship. A REAL man will attend professional counseling or seek some type of guidance if his personal shortcomings are creating distress for him and/or the woman he claims to love.

Myth 2: A REAL Man Is Proud and Does Not Apologize

The one thing that I have noticed about men is that we have a hard time saying, "I am sorry." Over the course of fourteen plus years of doing consultation and therapy, I have observed hundreds of women pour their hearts out and explain how and why their men hurt them. They even apologize for doing and saying things that upset or frustrated their men. After they finish speaking, I typically turn to their male counterparts and await a response.

Time after time, I watch men sit with a "what do you want me to say" look on their face and then they respond with solutions and justifications for their behavior, instead of saying, "I am sorry."

For some odd reason there are a lot of men who believe that a REAL man is a proud man who does not apologize." I agree that every man should be prideful; however, no man is too important to apologize to others, especially if they are deserving of an apology.

The negative impact: The Bible says that pride leads to disgrace (Proverbs 11:2); produces quarrels (Proverbs 13:10); leads to punishment (Proverbs 16:5); and destruction (Proverbs 16:18). Men who have too much pride will distance themselves from you and God.

The truth: A REAL man learns humility and is capable of giving compliments and lifting you up instead of tearing you down. A REAL man will apologize to you when he is wrong and will ask for your forgiveness. A REAL man realizes that his stubbornness is a sign of insecurity and will work to address his insecurity.

For many years I have observed and hung out with both married and single men and have noticed some very fundamental differences when it comes to their views about identity security and relationships. Married men who truly understand what it means to be a REAL man show signs of identity security. They are secure in their identities as husbands, heads of households, protectors, providers, lovers and compromisers. They do not feel that they have lost anything by being in committed relationships. In fact, most of them feel that they have gained something by committing and sharing their lives. They believe in compromising and appreciate the emotional fulfillment that comes with having someone in their lives who compliments them. They do not dread being vulnerable and often boast about showing affection to their women.

Single men, on the other hand, avoid commitment like a plague because they lack identity security. A strong sense of personal identity is important to developing intimate relationships. Men who have a poor sense of self and are afraid of being vulnerable tend to have less committed relationships and are more likely to suffer emotional isolation and loneliness. Guys who are great providers and protectors are great candidates, but because of their inability or unwillingness to be vulnerable and to demonstrate identity security, they are not qualified to be in a relationship.

Trust in Women

Trust in women is the second relationship quality that single men lack. Trust is an essential part of having healthy relationships and every woman desires to be with a man who trusts women. However, I believe that trust is difficult for most men because it has to do with how we feel. When we trust women we open ourselves up and expose our vulnerabilities. This is not easy for most guys, but some of us are willing to be vulnerable if we belief that we will not get hurt in the process of giving up our control.

Trust has many components to it and can be expressed in different ways and toward different people.

Have you ever met a man who appears to be confident and sure of himself when it comes to managing family challenges, career decisions and professional aspirations? As you monitor his mannerisms, he conducts himself in a very reassuring manner and does not demonstrate any signs of being untrusting. However, as you observe and interact with him over a period of time, you begin to notice that he has trust issues, especially when it comes to being involved in intimate relationships? On the surface he presents well and has confidence that makes him very appealing and desirable. He appears to be marriage material, but the more you interact with him the more you realize how untrusting of women he is.

I recently had a conversation about trust and women with a single colleague and I was overtaken by his lack of trust in women. As we talked, he mentioned that he would maintain separate bank accounts and would demand that he be able to do what he wants, when he wants. He expressed that most guys get lost in their relationships and marriages and he would not be one of them. He went on to say that he does not trust women and does not intend to lose his identity by entering into a relationship and allowing a woman to manipulate him. Every other sentence that came out of his month was centered on losing something, e.g. his manhood, freedom, money or peer respect. As I listened to the guy, I asked myself, "What the hell happened to him?"

I know a number of single good men who don't trust women and will do whatever they can to keep women at a distance, especially when it comes to being emotionally vulnerable. Some men might confide in women about issues related to their family and friends, but will not open up personally. This occurs because a number of men lack trust in women because their trust may have been violated during their childhood or in past relationships.

Here are few examples:

John (age 28): My mother left my father for another man when I was 12 years old. My father did not talk bad about my mother, but I did not like her much growing up. Women can be just as selfish as men. I don't trust them.

Eric (age 30): My first girlfriend hurt me when I was 15 years old and at that moment I made a promise that I would never be hurt like that again. I don't trust women. I am not trying to let a woman break my heart me again.

Rick (age 36): In my previous relationship I gave more than I received. I never thought someone who is suppose to love me could hurt me that bad. She cheated on me and told me to get over it.

In reading the aforesaid examples, you can see that men do not open back up too easily once our trust has been violated. When we hurt, we hurt! Given this, it is in your best interest to explore whether or not a man is trusting of women, because a man who has not resolved trust issues from childhood or past relationships will more than likely carry his distrust into future relationships. With this in mind, you need to make sure that you interact with men who have dealt with their trust issues.

Assessing a man's ability to trust is extremely important because men who are trusting behave differently than men who are untrusting. Men, who have trust in women, are typically free of suspicion and are more prone to cope in a positive manner when faced with adversity in their relationships. A trusting man will show faith in you because he knows that you will do right by him. If you were to leave your phone or email open, a trusting man will not feel a need to look through them. In comparison, men who lack trust in women are more prone to cope in a negative manner when faced with adversity in their relationships. They will not be open and will play mind games with you. Men who lack trust in women are often suspicious and will question your whereabouts—not in a caring manner, but in a "where the hell have you been" manner. He will probably surf through your belongings and start World War III if he finds some names or information that he is not familiar with.

You can tell if a man trusts you by listening to his tone, observing his behavior and watching his facial expression when he inquires about something that you have said or done.

If you are in a relationship and trust has been damaged, and you are not able to resolve the issue, seek professional help immediately. In all my years of doing therapy, I have never seen a healthy relationship work or last without trust. Trust sets the stage for love to prosper. Understand that trust must be present and mutually expressed in order to have a healthy relationship. If you meet a man who appears to be charming, gentle and sweet, but lacks trust in women, you should run like hell in the other direction. Regardless of what his reasons are for not trusting women, do not enter into a relationship with him until he resolves them. He might be a great candidate because he is honest about his views about women, but with unresolved trust issues, he is not qualified to be in a relationship.

Emotional Resilience

Emotional resilience is the third relationship quality that single men lack. Some men do not enter into relationships because we are not emotionally resilient. Emotional resilience can best be defined as a man's ability to bounce back after experiencing stress. Emotionally resilient men have the mental ability to return to a previous state of functioning after experiencing emotional trauma. Bouncing back and functioning in a healthy manner after experiencing heartbreak is not likely to occur with most men, especially without some kind of spiritual or mental health treatment. As previously stated, most men are not trained to cope with emotions, so when we are hurt it is difficult to bounce back. Heartbreaking trauma can be very debilitating for men.

When you come across a man who has had his heart broken, you should proceed with caution. There is a good chance that he has not fully recovered. Why do I say this? Men are not good at dealing with emotions. We are groomed to believe that emotions are not to be dealt with. Simply put, our growing pains are different than yours. For example, if a little boy falls down and scratches his knee, he is told that "big boys do not cry." In harsher words, he might be told to "stop crying you little punk;

crying is for girls." On the other hand, if a little girl falls down and scratches her knee, she is told it is okay to cry and is often held and kissed. I often get upset when I witness this behavior because *little boys who do not cry become men who do not cry.*

A large percentage of men who get hurt have scars that still need healing. I have talked to thousands of men who have told me that they are still hurting from painful relationship experiences that they had during their teen and young adult years. For most men, heartbreak is difficult to overcome because we lack the emotional aptitude needed to process our emotions in healthy ways. Withdrawing or expressing anger are the two responses that you will typically get from men, especially in times of emotional distress or sadness. The latter emotions are accepted and men are often given passes to demonstrate them instead of being challenged to express an array of emotions.

I believe that a good number of men lack emotional resiliency because we passively cope with pain, especially emotional pain associated with bad relationships. Men who cry are perceived to be weak and women typically do not embrace us if we show too much sensitivity. Therefore, men who are hurt are more likely to be scarred forever. If we have a bad relationship with a woman, we have to pretend that we are not hurting as much as she is. We walk around with open hurt wounds and receive band aide treatment instead of reconstructive heart surgery. Our scars eventually heal, but not in the proper manner. In talking to guys, I have learned that a man's first heartbreak will haunt him for the rest of his life if he does not have someone to help him understand and process the trauma. Time after time, we are pressured to be real men and are frequently reminded to maintain our manhood—"Do not act feminine."

Expressing sensitive or nurturing emotions or giving freely is not praised or encouraged. The pressure to maintain our masculinity and to remain strong often creates emotional roadblocks for us and feelings of remorse, forgiveness, sadness, and empathy are overshadowed by feelings of self-pity, anger, embarrassment, pride, and loss.

While both women and men experience emotional distress, men's coping styles are very passive in nature when it comes to dealing with emotions. As men we are repeatedly instructed to deny or minimize our emotions; therefore we often ignore and avoid dealing with them until they become unbearable.

Men who lack emotional resiliency and are not willing to develop active coping skills (more on this in chapter 13) are not qualified to be in relationships. Do not accept excuses. If a man wants to be with you, he will do what it takes to get you. Request that he attend counseling, seek spiritual guidance, talk to positive friends or do something if he has not resolved or effectively coped with previous or current emotional distress. Remember that emotionally resilient men see difficulties as temporary and are capable of bouncing back. Some men might be great candidates for relationships, but without emotional resiliency they are not qualified for the job.

Realistic Expectations

The inability to develop and sustain realistic expectations is the fourth relationship quality that single men lack. I recently facilitated a group discussion with fifteen single men and nearly every man who shared his thoughts about women and relationships had unrealistic expectations. When asked, "What do you want in a woman?" the majority of the guys reported that they are looking for a total package: a woman who is extremely attractive, humble, childless, down-to-earth, educated, professional, understands her worth and role, funny, feminine, spiritual and God-fearing, and freaky, but not in public. Most of the group discussion focused on these expectations/qualities and the majority of the guys stated that they want a woman who possess most of the qualities and are okay with waiting until they find her.

Randy, one of the most vocal guys in the group, blurted out, "I want a woman who looks like Halle Berry, cooks like she is from down south and is educated like the women in D.C. I need all of this. Also, she definitely has to be a professional woman who has money making potential like me."

After about thirty minutes into the discussion, I shifted the conversation to discuss the roles that they believe women and men should perform in relationships. One guy shouted, “I expect a woman to have my back in everything I do. I want a woman who will give her all, I mean 100%.” Another guy shouted, “I agree with him, I want a woman who will provide unwavering support, especially when I am down.” As the discussion heated up, the comments came one after the other and all started with “I want” and usually ended with something like “take care of me”.

While listening, I heard most of the guys talk a great deal about what they expect to receive from women, but did not hear them talk much about giving. When I pointed this out and reminded them that devotion to themselves will cause them to remain by themselves, I was told that it is difficult to shift from a “me mentality” to an “us mentality.” I was also told that women have to be willing to ride through the tough times with them and be patient.

I asked, “How do you guys expect to have healthy relationships if you are not willing to give just as much as you receive?”

One of the guys responded, “For a long time I did not give females an opportunity to get in my space and I still do not now. I don’t want too many people to get in my space because I don’t want to be hurt. I always have my defense up and I am always on defense regardless of how sweet a woman might be. I am not going to give a woman an opportunity to hurt my feelings or make me feel bad or ashamed because at the tail end I still have to support myself. So in the back of my mind, I am saying don’t give her everything, give her 75% because she is going to hurt you anyway."

As we talked more about their expectations, two common themes emerged: 1) they expect women to be generous and 2) they expect women to provide 100% unwavering support, but do not expect to be as generous to women and are only willing to give approximately 75% of unwavering support in return.

At the end of the group discussion, I explained that relationships are about giving and receiving and it is irrational to expect to receive 100% of unwavering support and only give 75% in return and expect to have a healthy relationship. I also explained that selfishness and self-centeredness has no place in relationships.

I ended the group session by saying, "Emotional intimacy, trust and mutual respect can only develop in relationships when two hearts are joined and both individuals are giving 100%." The guys concurred with me, but walked away with smirks on their faces.

One of the most difficult challenges we face as single men in regards to entering into and sustaining relationships, is learning how to be team players who give 100%. This transition is difficult for many single guys mainly because we develop lifestyles, habits and behaviors that are self-serving in nature. Also, a lack of identity security, trust in women and emotional resiliency will often lead to the development of unrealistic expectations about relationships. We want you to be close, but not too close.

There are a lot of single guys who avoid relationships or fail once we enter into them because our expectations are not realistic. Some people say that relationships are 50/50. I disagree. Relationships are about being willing to give 100% and understanding that some days 50% is all that can be given. Some days we fall short and need help—that is the beauty of having a partner. The willingness to give 100% is what makes relationships work.

If you meet a guy who expects to receive more than he is willing to give and desires to be with a perfect woman, let him know that he is a great candidate because he knows exactly what he wants, but remind him that he is not qualified to be in a relationship, especially with you.

Part Two

Why Is It So Difficult For Single Good Men to Abandon Singlehood

Chapter 4

Singlehood Is Widely Accepted: Marriage Is Optional

Unfortunately, marriage is not rated as highly as it once was in our society. In this day and age, a lot of women and men feel that marriage is optional. Within the past two years statistics about singlehood have increased drastically. According to the U.S. Census Bureau "America's Families and Living Arrangements: 2010", there are 99.6 million unmarried people over the age 18 in the United States, representing nearly 44% of the adult population. And for every 100 unmarried women there are 88 unmarried men.

The reasons for the rise in these alarming statistics about singlehood can be linked to the demographical and economical changes that have occurred as a result of the industrial and technological revolution and Women's Movement. Of the three changes that have taken place over the years, the Women's Movement has had a more profound impact on the marriage institution. As women attain more education and seek job security, marriage is being delayed. This shift has impacted the thinking and behavior of single good men because they often do not anticipate that they will meet a "good" woman who is ready for marriage.

Women are making more money than ever before in history; therefore marriage no longer provides the financial security for women that it once did. In fact, many single good women that I have spoken to over the years, informed me that they also dread and toil with the idea of marriage because they are afraid of losing assets that they have acquired as successful professional women.

Single good men, just like you, are constantly reevaluating the need to get married, especially during their mid twenties and thirties because they are focusing on and trying to accomplish professional goals. Making money, living comfortable lifestyles and securing one's future has taken precedence over the desire to get married.

Many men and women say that they would like to get married, but their actions are not consistent with their desires. Both men and women are embracing singlehood and are living lifestyles that do not limit their freedom. And unfortunately, the institution of marriage is no longer viewed as an important milestone in the lives of most young adults—marriage is optional.

I recently had a conversation with one of my female friends about the institution of marriage and I asked, "Do you believe that marriage is important?"

She looked at me with a stunned look on her face and said, "Of course, but a lot of women, especially Black women do not see marriage as a viable option. There are not that many good men out here so I am just doing me. If a man comes along and sweeps me off of my feet, then I will get married. I am not in any rush. My career is more important right now anyway. I enjoy hanging out with my girls and dating causally. Marriage is important, but it's just not for me right now, plus I do not have to be married to be happy or have a family."

As I listened to her, I reflected on other conversations that I have had with hundreds of women who felt and thought the same way. After she finished speaking, I told her that she would probably never get married. She looked at me cross-eyed and said, "Excuse me. What do you mean?"

Ladies, it is simple. Your mindset and attitude about marriage sets the stage for how you will live your life and how men will respond to you. If you view marriage as being optional, your actions and behaviors will be consistent with your view and men will treat you as an option. Men are good at picking up on women who feel hopeless about marriage. We pursue women who talk about marriage, but do not truly believe that it is a viable option. We understand that you will not pressure us to marry you because you are ambivalent about being married and place more value on being single.

We use your ambivalence about marriage and acceptance of singlehood as a weapon against you. We observe your emotional distress as you watch the divorce rate rise. We listen to the distraught conversations you have about marriage with your girlfriends and family members. And, we occasionally provide you with information that highlights that millions of men and women are deciding not to marry, but are living happy lifestyles with benefits.

With a little charm, we convince you to believe that marriage is important, but it's not for you or us. Men advocate for loving you without requirements other than offering you good sex and the reassurance of knowing that marriage might be on the horizon if we stay together.

Single men are reaping the benefits of being a part of a sexual revolution that involves high rates of co-habitation, causal dating and unlimited sex. The "get all the sex you can " mindset appears to be the driving force behind the desire to remain single for a large percentage of men and women. Many women and men believe that sex before marriage is a prerequisite to having a good relationship. Discussions about marriage can be found on most relationships blogs, but people are not changing their ways, especially when it comes to managing their sexual desires and energy.

Erica, a devoted blogger, shared this comment:

> I've been pondering the dynamics of marriage and relationships in America for a few weeks as I've been getting to know some people. I'm discouraged that sex is the focus of most things in society and the root cause of so much destruction. If more people could control themselves, just think about how life might be different. Fewer unwanted pregnancies, less crime, and maybe people would get married first before having kids. Anyway, it's a serious matter, but it's kinda making me horny. Lol

The idea of settling down and marrying is becoming more frightening for single good men and women because singlehood is widely accepted. Sexual pleasure is prevailing over traditional values associated with marriage. One of the guys I play basketball with recently told me that he enjoys being single because he is capable of selecting from a diverse pool of women who are okay with having casual sex. Another guy told me that he has difficulty abandoning singlehood because there is no pressure to get married—women accept the fact that he will not commit or be serious with them. Both guys stated that they have a "get sex first, get married afterwards" mentality.

It is without doubt that marriage as an option or back-up plan has gained widespread acceptance during the twenty-first-century. Marriage is perceived to be too difficult and single good men are choosing to remain single. Everywhere you look, people are divorcing and the tabloids are filled with disparaging stories about bad marriages. This unfortunate phenomenon has significantly caused millions of married-minded single men to view marriage negatively.

As a single man, I can appreciate the benefits of singlehood; however as a marital therapist I do believe that marriage has benefits that are equally as rewarding. I provide eighty percent of the marital counseling in my office and get to see the good aspects of marriage as well. For example, married people have lifetime companionship and reap the benefits of two incomes, two minds and unwavering support for each other when confronted with adversity. But most importantly, marriage makes God happy because He ordained it.

In Sum, single men have difficulty with abandoning singlehood because it is widely accepted and marriage is optional. Society as a whole does not place value in the marriage institute anymore and single good men are going along for the ride.

Chapter 5

Influenced by Bad Role Models: Married, but Single

"Can married men be addicted to the single lifestyle? Why do some married men act single?" These are questions that I receive from married and single women regularly who are baffled about men's behavior.

In talking with married men, I sometimes, hear them say that being single was the best time in their life and some still fantasize about singlehood. Rarely, do I hear them talk about their marriages and if they do, I often do not hear the positive aspects. This occurs primarily because most men often do not share sensitive stories or emotions with the women in their lives, so sharing with another man is definitely out of the question. Men are very private for the most part, unless we are bragging about our accomplishments, arguing about sports or displaying some kind of hostility toward somebody who upset us. Rarely, will you hear a married man talk about how beautiful, kind and intelligent his wife is to another man unless they are in church, at a relationship seminar or attending a marriage retreat.

Single good men who have a desire to be married constantly search for answers and information about marriage. It is sad to say, but a large percentage of married men encourage single guys to remain single. This is not true of all married men, but a large percentage of married men do not appreciate their wives in the early stages of their marriages. In many of my encounters with married men, I often walk away feeling discouraged about marriage. The conversations we have about marriage are scary as hell. They make marriage sound like they are serving jail sentences and often describe their wives as being wicked and cruel wardens who have total control over them and their relationship.

Consider exhibit A

Text Message from a Married Colleague

Married guy: Thinking about getting out tonight. What are you up to?

Me: Nothing much. Just relaxing!

Married guy: I am going to hit you up later so we can hang out. Maybe go shoot some pool or hit a spot.

Me: Cool. Just let me know. Hit me up later tonight.

Married guy: Man's it around 10 p.m. and I don't think I am going to make it.

Me: Why not?

Married guy: My wife wants me to spend time with her; she got an attitude. Man you should stay single so you don't have to deal with this stuff.

This is just one example of how some married men view their wives and marriage. And, in response to what some married men perceive to be hard times in their relationships, many still act single. Some married men cheat and treat their wives like second class citizens. They come and go as they see fit and brag about being able to do what they want and when they want. Hanging out every other weekend until 3 and 4 a.m. is not viewed as being inconsiderate or disrespectful.

I occasionally hang out with a few single colleagues at local clubs, bars and jazz spots and I am often perplexed by the number of married men who still hang out in clubs and pick up women on a regular basis. I am also perplexed by the number of married men who talk about women as if they are not married.

Consider exhibit B

Text Message from a Married Colleague

Me: What's up brother? I'm in Arizona until Sunday celebrating my birthday. Let me know if you can meet up.

Married guy: Hey man where are you in Arizona? I can get out. My wife does not question me.

Me: Phoenix.

Married guy: Do you leave on Sunday or Monday?

Me: Sunday.

Married guy: I can take you to some hot spots. The ladies are down and have no problem with showing a brother a good time. I get something new every time I go out … lol. We have a lot of pretty women down here. Really!!! I will hit you later.

Me: Cool.

Married guy: Most definitely! My boy James moved here from New York and he is always fucking with the women lol. It's rough for a married dude trying to act right lmao.

Me: U can do it.

Married guy: Man I know, but I need God's help lol. That's always been my nemesis: booty lmao.

After reading this, you are probably saying to yourself, "single men can chose to listen to and hang around more positive role models—men who value their wives and marriage."

I agree, and I encourage other single men to do exactly what you are thinking—find good counsel. However, I can count on one hand the number of times I have had conversations with men outside of therapy who willingly disclose how they truly feel about their wives and marriage. Given this, single good men have a lot to process when it comes to women, relationships and marriage. Some single men want to be married but are not, and some married men want to be single but cannot.

The decision to abandon singlehood is probably played over and over in the minds of single good men at least a million times; however, the images we see are often not good. The divorce rate is over 50% in the United States. Men and women are not honoring their vows anymore and are walking away from their marriages like never before. And although, some married men set bad examples, single men are not totally discouraged about marriage because of married men's behavior. There are a lot of factors that impacts men's difficulty with abandoning singlehood and observing married men act single is just one of them. In Chapter 8—*The X-Factor: Women's Behavior*, I provide some insight into how women play a role into single men's difficulty in regards to abandoning singlehood.

Chapter 6

Single Good Men Are Rare Commodities and Have Nice Benefits

Am I A Commodity?

The dating scene is a playground for single good men who are in their early to mid thirties; successful, educated; childless and financially comfortable. Men who meet these criteria typically reap the benefits of being able to choose from a large selection of women ranging from young to old, unattractive to attractive, uneducated to educated, slim to thick and down-to-earth to high-maintenance. They realize that they are rare commodities and make it known that they have options because there are plenty of women who are searching for them.

Men who belong to this perceived "elite" clan definitely have great benefits, especially Black men. According to Best Black Dating Sites, there are only 3 Good Black men for every 100 Black women.

In talking to single men who are "rare commodities," I learned that single men who reside in certain geographical regions or areas perceive that they have better benefits than others. For example, single men residing in the Washington, D.C. and Atlanta areas reported that they have more "quality" to pick from than single men who reside in cities in the Mid-west and South. Men from the D.C. and Atlanta areas talked extensively about being able to date women with law degrees, MBAs and PhDs who are also freaky. They boasted about dating women with higher salaries and growth potential. They bragged about having the option to date above and below their economic status.

Many single men say they want to get married and abandon singlehood, but the benefits are too great. Being single and a rare commodity means that men can do whatever they want and do not have to consult with anyone; being single means that men do not have to sacrifice or compromise; being single means you can flirt with and date multiple women; being single means that men do not have to worry about some else's emotional well-being; being single means that men can get as much sex as they want without any strings attached; and being single means that men do not have to cope with relationship stressors.

Of all the benefits that are associated with being a single good man and a rare commodity, the three that were reported to be most rewarding according to my poll is as follows: 1) they can have unlimited and unattached sex; 2) avoid the real and/or perceived *stressors* associated with commitment or marriage and; 3) enjoy the perks associated with being placed on a pedestal.

Generally speaking, most single good men have difficulty with abandoning singlehood because they love the benefits that single men receive, especially single men who are rare commodities. Some single men truly embrace their singleness and the associated benefits. A 31-year-old bachelor from St. Louis, Missouri reported, "You look at yourself as a high commodity and you should. There is nothing wrong with this and I think women should look at themselves as high commodities as well. I am not going to just settle for anything. There is a difference between comprising and settling. I'm going to seek what I want and you should too."

A 35-year-old bachelor in D.C. shared similar thoughts, "When it comes down to whether or not I think I am a rare commodity for this area or for women in general, the answer is yes, by far. How many African American men do you know that are somewhat successful? I am a single male and don't have any children. Not to say that if I did have children I would not be a rare commodity. I just do not at this time. What it all boils down to is that so many women see this and say, 'why aren't you married and how can I become a part of your life.' For me the more I become a rare community, the more that I am able to provide for a woman. Once I get to the point where I do want to be in a full time relationship and decide to get married, you better believe that it will be with a woman who also is a rare commodity."

Lastly, a 37-year-old bachelor from Atlanta shared his thoughts about being single and a rare commodity: "Being a rare commodity is a special place to be because women have no expectations. So they do not expect you to love them like the everyday Joe because they put you on a higher pedestal. A lot of time men like to stand up there and I am not any different. I like to stand on a pedestal too. However, a lot of women come at me wrong. They be like 'I can buy my own dinner and I can do this and that' because they think that I expect them to be where I am at in life and that is not true. So I am a rare commodity almost by force. Women put me in that box and sometimes I just like being jack."

I personally think that a lot of single guys, who view themselves as being rare commodities, feel empty on the inside and the quest to fulfill that void is met by changing women and convincing themselves that singlehood is not so bad. However, every single man that I interviewed from the East Coast, Mid-West and West Coast appeared to be satisfied with his lifestyle and spoke highly about the benefits of singlehood. For example, Mark, a 28-year-old bachelor from California, had this to say, "The benefit of being single is that you get to go shopping everyday. [laughing] It's like a buffet and you get to be particular. When you get to a certain age, you like quality. When you were probably twenty-one you were okay with buying a rug from Target that was probably seven dollars, but when you are thirty-five you go to Pier 1 because you want that forty dollar rug that is going to last a few years. So that is the thing about being single, you get to pick and chose height, weight, size and shape."

Steve, a 34 year-old actor added, "Are there benefits to being a single good man, yes there are, but most of the time I don't think we take full advantage of them. I'm not a NBA player, you know what I mean, but I was asked this question just last week. I met this bad chick and she asked me why I was single. I told her I just am because everybody wants me to be in a relationship."

In discussing the benefits of being single with men from various cities throughout America, I have concluded that being a single good man with great qualities is without question a benefit that is highly desired among men in the United States. Abandoning singlehood is difficult because a part of being single is being selfish—some single good men feel that they can do whatever the hell they want to do and women will allow it.

Chapter 7

Men Like to Take the Path of Least Resistance: Why Commit If We Don't Have Too?

Some of you often wonder why men hang around, but never commit. This may come across as being harsh, but "Why should we commit if we do not have to?" asks Allen, a 38 year-old business owner. Allen went on to say, "Single men don't have to commit if they are not given that option. Some women are looking at their watches and saying it's about that time and some women are not. A lot of men don't have too. Like you mentioned earlier, some single men are rare commodities and they know it. So if you don't have to do anything, why would you?"

Reading this must be difficult for you, but this is a reality because you allow it. I apologize; let me reframe this. Reading this must difficult for you, but this is a reality because men decide to travel this path and you choose to be a part of their journey. I reframed my comment because I want you to understand that you are not the primary cause for this kind of behavior. You do play a role in influencing men's decision to commit or not, but only as a contributor (more on this in the next Chapter).

Most single men do not commit because we like to take the path of least resistance. Taking the path of least resistance means that men will take the easiest way to reach our aims and solve problems, especially in relationships. We engage in this behavior to help save time and, most importantly, to reserve emotional energy.

Unfortunately, a large percentage of men that I see in therapy and in my consultation business tell me that they got married or jumped into a relationship because it was the easiest thing to do at the time. This is not to say that they were not in love, but they took the path of least resistance. You must understand what the path of least resistance means to men. This is difficult to figure out because every man operates differently in regards to traveling the path of least resistance. For example, if marrying you will shut you up and take the pressure off, then some men will do just that—path of least resistance. If men can get sex without commitment, then some men will do just that—path of least resistance.

In *Act Like A Lady, Think Like A Man*, Steve Harvey suggested that you set standards and deploy a ninety-day rule in order to get the respect you deserve and to determine if a man is worth your time and benefits. He recommended that you ask men the following five questions before you get in too deep: 1) what are your short-term goals; 2) what are your long-term goals; 3) what are your views on relationships; 4) what do you think about men; and 5) how do you feel about me? He also provided a list of things you could do with your man during your ninety-day plan. I like the questions and suggestions that he made and believe that they can help with assessing the commitment issue and determining if a man is truly interested and right for you. However, I think that Steve Harvey forgot to tell you to ask two very important questions: 1) will you talk to a professional about our relationship? and 2) what are your thoughts about seeking pre-marital or on-going therapy if warranted?

These questions will definitely get most men worked up because men are very private beings and do not like talking about their business, especially to strangers. Talking with you and going along with a ninety-day plan is easier than you think for most men; however, talking to others about our feelings, thoughts and backgrounds is more difficult.

I am not suggesting that you try to make a man's life hell by asking him to do things just to be doing them. However, I have found that when it comes to relationships, men often do not put forth the same effort and commitment as you do.

You can ask your man all kinds of questions and make him wait ninety days in order to assess his worthiness, but I would encourage you to pay more attention to his behavioral tendencies: 1) does he have a tendency to take the easy way out?; 2) does he have a tendency to select easy solutions over challenging solutions?; and 3) does he have a tendency to put forth whatever effort is needed to get the highest reward from his relationships?

Knowing and understanding your man's behavioral tendencies will help you determine if he is worth starting a relationship with. Also understanding his tendencies will help you determine if he will jump ship when things get difficult. Women who take the time to learn about their men's behavioral tendencies are successful at walking away before getting caught up. They learn that there is a difference between getting a man and getting a quality man who is willing to work.

In sum, some single men have difficulty with abandoning singlehood, because they do not want to invest in women by putting forth the patience, effort or commitment needed to sustain a relationship—like Allen said, "Why commit, if we don't have too?"

Chapter 8

The X-Factor: Women's Behavior Do Women Influence Men's Decisions to Remain Single?

No man can deny the power of a woman. When God created man He knew men could not survive without companionship, so He gave us you, the most precious gift to mankind. God equipped you with gifts that astonish men. You are capable of giving life to the world, comforting the sick, giving moral support, showing compassion, loving unconditionally, standing up against injustice, bearing hardships, carrying burdens, and holding happiness, love and joy.

Simply stated you are special.

Now that I got that out of the way; back to the issue at hand.

Men were created to have dominion over the earth; to rule as conquerors and to lead our wives and children. From a biblical stance, God created man to influence and lead. However, from the beginning of time, women have had the ability to significantly influence men's behavior, but not always in a good manner. The story of Adam and Eve clearly illustrates the influence and power that women have over men. As you learned in Bible study, Adam disobeyed God because he did not completely embrace and understand his role as the head and allowed Eve to persuade him to do what he was not supposed to do—eat from the Tree of Knowledge.

Now, stick with me as I walk you through the chain of events that unfolded in the Garden of Eve.

On one nice and sunny day, a cool and smooth talking serpent approached Eve and told her that she should eat from the Tree of Knowledge because it would make her be more like God. The serpent also reassured Eve that eating from the tree would not lead to death. Eve hesitated initially, but after thinking about it for a little while, she decided to eat from the tree. After Eve ate, she shared with Adam, who ate as well. Both Adam and Eve knew they had done wrong and decided to hide from God. When approached by God and asked, "What happened?", Adam blamed Eve for giving him the fruit and Eve blamed the serpent for seducing her.

I mention the story of Adam and Eve because it illustrates how women can and do influence men. The story also highlights some of the challenges men and women face in our ability to develop and sustain healthy relationships. Relationships between women and men will never work smoothly as long as individuals allow seduction to prevail over good judgment, lack understanding of their roles, and fail to take responsibility for their actions.

Up until this point, I have explored and informed you about some of the psychological and behavioral issues that influence why single good men decide to remain single. Now it is time to shift gears and talk about the one factor that significantly influences men's decision to remain single—your behavior.

In conducting interviews with single men about their difficulty with abandoning singlehood, every one of them mentioned that women's behavior is among the top five reasons that influence their decisions to remain single. When I asked them to expound, I was told that women are typically placed into six categories based on their behavior. Here are the categories:

Category #1—Deceptive Women

Deceptive women play games with men by either lying or trying to persuade us to believe things that are not true. Some women engage in this kind of behavior with the intent of gaining an advantage over men. The advantage can be either financial or emotional in nature and the deceitful woman always has her own advantage in mind.

"Identifying deceptive women is difficult for men because some women are so deceptive that men cannot tell the difference between women who are truly genuine from those who are deceptive," Trina, twenty-four year old hairstylist.

The quickest way to contribute to a man's lack of trust in women is to deceive him. Men do not like to deal with women who pretend to be interested in us but are faking. We, as men, love to be promised great things by women and thrive off attention. However, should we find out that a woman had no intentions of living up to her promises, we automatically go into "I don't trust women" defense mode.

Deceit is one of the main reasons why so many single good men do not trust women and decide to remain single. Once deceit occurs, trust vanishes and mistrust takes over.

Story #1—Mario

> I will never forget Erica. When I first met her she told me that she really liked me and was interested in having a serious relationship. We hung out a lot and she occasionally spent nights at my place. I remember coming home early one day and heard her telling her girl that she is dating me because she is looking for financial stability. She also told her girl that she was going to use me for money, break me down and leave me because she felt that I was too damn arrogant.

> For some time, she had me believing that she was truly interested in me. She knew that she did not like me from jump start, but entered into my circle anyway. Never again will I trust another … bitch.

Story #2—Andy

> Deceit is a motherfucker. My girl Kim told me that she was pregnant, so I proposed to her. I did not propose just because she was pregnant, I truly loved her. I told her that I was not ready for marriage yet, but wanted to do right by her. As we made plans to move forward with our lives together, I started hanging around her more. About five months passed before things went south. I received an anonymous phone call from some dude who claimed that he got Kim pregnant. He told specific details of how and where he hooked with Kim. I did not want to believe him, but he knew things about Kim's body that someone could only know if they were intimately involved with her. Man, I was disappointed and mad. I approached Kim and asked, "Is that my child inside you?" Kim looked stunned and began to cry. Kim replied, "I let you believe that it was your baby because I did not want to hurt you. I did not mean to be deceptive, but I felt trapped. Plus I did not want to raise a child by myself.

All forms of deceit, whether spiteful or unintentional, are harmful. Knowing something is false and then leading someone down that path is very hurtful. Believe it or not, men hurt more than you think. Some men can forgive women who say things that are not truthful, especially if we do not feel a true connection with you. However, we have a much harder time dealing with deceit when it comes from women who we are connected to and/or care about.

Category #2—Desperate Women

Men do not like dealing with desperate women and often decide to remain single in order to avoid drama queens. Some of you want to be in relationships so bad, that you act too damn anxious. I personally get annoyed by women who go out with me on Monday and demand a ring on Friday. Unfortunately, this happens to a lot of single good men and sometimes I would like to scream, "Chill the hell out, enjoy the date and let God work for you." However, being the gentleman that I am I often say, "Just relax and God will send you a king soon."

I hate to say this, but the older some women get, the more desperate some of you all appear. Some women might disagree and defend their desperate behavior by declaring, "I know what I want and do not want. Plus I do not have time for games."

I did not mention the "age and desperation" correlation to start a debate or to upset you; I simply mentioned it because some of the men who I interviewed view and label older women (35 years of age and older) as desperate because some of you jump on the fast track toward marriage before you get to know a man.

Story #1—James

> I went on a dinner date with this fine young lady and I was totally impressed with her demeanor. She was easy going and down-to-earth. After we finished eating dinner, I asked her if I could see her again because I really enjoyed her company. She looked at me and said, "I don't know what you are looking for, but I am not looking to date casually. I did that while I was in college and in my early twenties. I am not looking to get married anytime soon, but I at least want to be in a serious relationship. If we hang out again, I need know where this is going. You look like marriage material."

After she finished speaking I was shocked. I asked for another date and was given her lifetime relationship plan. I did not mind the straightforwardness, but her undertone was not good. I felt like I was in a Desperate House Wife scene. I politely thanked her for sharing her thoughts and took her home. As I drove away from her home I accidentally deleted her telephone number."

Story #2—Romeo

> My late date was very interesting. She had an overwhelming need to tell me of how great she was. She talked consistently about how she could take care of business in the kitchen and did not mind pleasing her man in the bedroom. She talked about being submissive and expressed dissatisfaction for women who do not know how

> to please men. She told me that she would treat me a like a King if I was her man. And lastly, she told me that she is single because most men can't handle being with a real woman who is confident and knows what she wants. She ended by telling me that she has only been single for a short period and expects to be in another relationship soon. Now mind you, I was somewhat impressed, until I came to my senses and realized that this was our very first date. This woman was desperate. She submitted an application and wanted to be hired on the spot.

Does either of the descriptions above describe you? If you are not sure, let me to help you out. You are a desperate woman if you meet the following criteria:

1. You are a lifetime dater and love being in relationships.

2. You establish and maintain strict deadlines about relationships, commitment, marriage and pregnancy and will include any good man into your plan.

3. You often display very anxious behavior around men and dread being single for extended periods of time.

4. You are extremely nice and typically go along with what men want—impressing men is important to you.

5. You consistently seek affection and obsess about commitment.

Please do not take offense and shoot the messenger if you are a desperate woman.

The sad thing about some desperate women is that some of you will probably make good wives. However, you do not know how to let the chips to fall where they must. You cannot treat every good man as if he is the one. As I mentioned earlier, most men including myself get annoyed as hell when you size us up to be your husband without even getting to know us. There is nothing wrong with letting a man know where you stand and laying out your expectations, but hold back on the desperation talk. You do not have to sell yourself. Plus, some men know what we want and don't want, just like you, so please be tactful and monitor what comes out of your mouth.

As you can see based on the few responses listed above, most men will not hang out with or get to know a desperate woman, so I encourage you to enjoy the date and keep a level head—no marriage talk on the first date. Only three things happen to desperate women—they get hurt, taken advantage of, or left alone to prey on other men. As a single man, I strongly advise you to reevaluate your approach if you fall into this category—this is hard to say, but you scare the hell out of us.

Category #3—Damaged Women

Some men remain single because they do not want to deal with women who have been damaged from previous relationships. Women who are still hurting from their previous relationship have a tendency to bring baggage with them into their new relationship. A bitter and hurt woman is not easy to deal with and most men would prefer not to get involved.

Story #1—Eddie

> Most women think that there are no good men out here because they have been hurt in past relationships. My girl brought a lot of baggage with her. I am not saying that I am perfect and don't make mistakes, but I do not hold her accountable for the actions of other women. She is different! I am constantly reminded of how the other guy did this and did that to her. I try to be sensitive, but I have a hard enough time trying to make up for my own mistakes, so I sure in the hell can't make up for another man's mistakes. After about three months of hearing about past drama, I jumped ship. I can be miserable by myself. They say misery likes company; well I don't need or want that kind of company.

Story #2—Ronald

> I met Stacey, a single mother of two children, through a mutual friend. When I first met Stacey, I thought she was a good catch because she was a good woman. She took care of her business,

> her children and was a trustworthy woman. I liked her nurturing and down-to-earth spirit. She was very good with her children. I did not see any concerning flaws until we started dating seriously.
>
> I remember when the drama started. I asked Stacey to marry me after dating for one year. On the day I proposed, her emotional issues began to surface. She went off on a tangent about how she has been hurt before by the father of her children and is not going to go through that again. I was shocked because I had done everything in my power to reassure Stacey that I would not abandon or hurt her. Plus we had this conversation at least forty times within the past year. I suggested that we seek counseling on several occasions, but Stacey did not feel that she needed any help and told me, "I am a little scared, but you need to understand that I will probably struggle with this fear for the rest of my life." Although I cared about Stacey, I was not willing to subject myself to a lifetime of misery. She was holding me in hostage mode because of what some other man did to her. I called off the engagement and moved on. Love lost, but peace of mind gained.

I realize that it is difficult to recover from pain or hurt, but I can assure you that no man wants to deal with unresolved grief or pain. Now you might say, "A real man will stand by his woman and help her work through her problems." I agree, partially. I can tell you from personal and professional experience that a damaged soul is like living without an identity. I have observed men try to modify their actions to provide comfort and security, but have had little success. A man can love a woman, but a woman will not get over her pain until she is ready and willing to be loved. Unresolved bitterness and pain can keep men at a distance—who wants to be with a damaged woman?

Category #4—Independent Women

If I meet one more woman who tells me that she can open her own car door, pay her own bills, fix things around her house and basically screw herself, I am going to commit myself to a mental health ward. Excuse me for being somewhat traditional, but I do not do well with the new twenty-first-century women—women who are too dam independent.

I remember when women used to allow men to do things for them because they desired, demand and respected chivalry. Nowadays, women are quick to remind us that they "do not need a man." I agree that you do not need a man, but if you want a man, stop acting so damn independent. What do I mean?

I am not suggesting that you bow down to a man and act as if you cannot do anything for yourself. I am simply suggesting that you allow a man to be man. Respect what he brings to the table. I know you have heard this a million times, but hearing something and understanding it is different. Understand that some men take great pride in treating women like Queens. And I am not talking about buying you material things.

There is nothing more attractive to man than being with a woman who knows her role and worth. A woman who knows her worth and role will allow her man to support her and will support him in return. Coretta Scott King exemplified this behavior and set the standard for women like Michelle Obama to follow.

Stop screaming, "I can do it" and start screaming, "I can do it, but it would be nice if you helped or did it for me." The "I Am an Independent Woman" persona is not attractive at all.

Story #1—Ronald

> I met Angie at social event for young professional adults. We started hanging out on a regular basis shortly after meeting at the social. Every time we hung out she bragged about how she makes just as much money as men do and holds a high position in her organization. Initially, her boastfulness bothered me, but I ignored it because I figured that she talked that way to either impress me or to remind me that she does not need me. I did not mind mingling with Angie because I like confident women who are capable of taking care of themselves. I think it is sexy. However, as time passed Angie insisted that we split the bills whenever we would go out to eat. I informed Angie that I did not mind paying for her occasionally because I enjoyed her company. Angie told me that she has been doing things for

> herself for so long that she does not know how to accept chivalry.

Story #2—Ronald

> I recently met this young lady for a walk in the park and she went on and on about how she could do this for herself and do that for herself so I asked her why would she need a man. She looked at me and replied, "You want me to be honest. Other than fulfilling my sexual needs, I would have to think about it. My father taught me to be very independent, so I don't require a man to do much for me." That was our first and last date.

Most women get defensive when men start talking about the "independent woman" issue. I personally believe that women who struggle with this issue do not understand their roles. A woman can be self-sufficient without making a man feel unwanted. Furthermore, a real man does not want you to feel inadequate or inferior so that he can feel empowered. Stroking a man's ego is not a bad thing, especially if he is stroking yours in return.

Learn to humble yourself and accept chivalry. I can tell you that there is nothing more annoying to a man than going out with a woman who brags about being able to take care of herself, but she never reaches for the bill after eating dinner. Sometimes I would like to say, "If you are that damn independent, then pick up the tab." Now some women don't have a probably with this, but that is not my point. I know you all are capable of doing things for yourselves. That is easy. The challenge for most independent women is developing the willingness and ability to allow men to cater to you.

With all the game playing going on, I realize that it's hard to let your guard down and to accept kind gestures from men, but this independent woman thing is too much. The "independent woman" concept is anti-relationship in my opinion. The last time I checked, human existence has sustained throughout history because men and women continue to rely on each other. Sharing and depending on each other is what makes relationships blossom, not individuality.

The song "Independent Women" was a national anthem for women in 2000 and ignited a spark among millions. Women all around the world developed the courage to step out on their own with confidence, but as they say all good things must come to an end—I guess Beyonce got tired of being an independent woman (go Jay-Z).

Category #5—Jump-Off Women

This category of women has supernatural power over single good men. I was at a comedy show in St. Louis and I heard this comedian, define a *Jump-Off Woman* as such: a woman who a man can tell anything to and she will let him jump off into her. He also mentioned that Jump-Offs are usually first cousins of

Gold-Diggers. I tried not to laugh, but every man in the audience was laughing hysterically, especially the single guys.

The comedian went on to say that jump-off women are like nymphomaniacs, they love to have a lot of sex and as often as possible. According to the comedian, jump-off women are mostly impressed with a man's title and want nothing more than to be in the physical presence of a successful, ambitious and attractive man.

As I heard the comedian talk about this category of women, I was somewhat bothered because there are millions of women who fall into this category and they make it easy for single good men to remain single.

Story #1—Pete

> I met Sandra at my boy's birthday party on Friday and I hit her Sunday. She stopped by the house late Sunday evening and we were having sex within two hours of her arrival. She told me that she was impressed with the way I carried myself. She told me that she is only attracted to men who have their heads on right. I could not believe that she was that easy. Usually the successful women try to run game and hold out, but not her. Man the world has changed drastically. Some women do not have a problem with giving it up.

Story #2—Anthony

> What single man in his right mind would turn down easy sex? Just last Saturday I met this young lady at Home Depot and she told me that she likes guys who are handy. We sparked up a conversation and I asked her out. She agreed and we decided to meet on Tuesday evening for dinner.
>
> Tuesday came around and we met at a nice restaurant. Nothing too fancy or expensive, but very nice. We had great discussions about various topics (relationships, politics, etc.) and I was truly impressed with her. At the end of our date, she asked if I wanted to go back to her place for light refreshments. Of course, I agreed. Shortly, after we enjoyed some chocolate covered strawberries, we pleasured ourselves by having some hot and careless sex. Man, jump-offs are God's gifts to single men.

If you fall into this category, please seek some counsel. I do not mean to judge you, but your behavior will never provide you with the kind of happiness that you deserve. Having casual sex might fulfill a sexual need for you and your partner, but you will never be respected by a man. Single men might love spending time with you, but don't even think about commitment.

Category #6—High-Maintenance Women

High maintenance women are usually attractive women who serve as good trophies for single men, but are too expensive to keep long-term. They typically have perfectionist tendencies and spend an excessive amount of time, money and energy trying to maintain a perfect appearance. Their nails, makeup and hair must be on point all the time (weekly) and they will do whatever is needed to maintain their youth, feminine and beauty. They are more likely to have surgical procedures (breast implants, skin treatments, etc.) performed and normally view men as money making machines.

High maintenance women are very selective in who they date and are often perceived to be boo-jay. They expect their men to drive certain cars, live in certain areas and have unlimited assets. This category of women can consist of the highly educated, professional women or uneducated ghetto women. Their primary goal is to find a man who can assist them with developing or sustaining a fabulous lifestyle. Most of the women that fall into this category feel that they are entitled to being happy and usually pressure men into buying them expensive gifts, cars, clothing, and jewelry. However, some of the women can take care of themselves, but they will not entertain men who cannot take care of them or keep them happy.

Most single men who like "average women" typically date high maintenance women for show case purposes and rarely take them serious or commitment to them. Even guys who are financially well-off and can afford high maintenance women often report that they do not commit to them on a long-term basis because they do not like to deal with the personality quirks.

Story #1—Tim

> I briefly dated this female who was high maintenance. She was very attractive, but acted Boojay as hell. My sisters and aunts did not like her because she acted as if she was too good to interact with them.
>
> Her father owned a couple of clothing stores so she was used to getting what she wanted. Whenever we would go out to eat she ordered the most expensive food, wine and dessert, but she never offered to pay for anything. On an average, I would spend two to three hundred dollars each time we went out to dine (sometimes twice a week). I remember asking her why she always chooses fancy restaurants and she told me that she does not eat at cheap restaurants. After hanging out with her for a few months, I realized that I could not afford her company. I mentioned that I might need to break things off and she told me that she did not think that I could afford her anyway. I was not mad at all. My savings account increased with the loss.

Story #2—Peter

> I did not know Jennifer would be so high maintenance when we first met. She was a nice looking young lady, but did not come from "old money." She grew up in a middle-class household in the suburbs. So I was amazed by her unwavering desire to shop at expensive stores. Nordstrom was one of her favorite stores. I remember going shopping with her and she asked me to buy her a hand bag. I did not mind, so I told her yes. She walked down the aisle and came back with a Lanvin Hand Bag that cost $3,685.00.
>
> I am not going to tell you what I said to her, but I will tell you that we did not talk again after that day.

As a woman, you have the ability to influence men in many ways and everything that you do significantly impacts us in one way or another. Everything you do, matters to us. We might not tell you, but believe me, your actions have power.

Men place women in categories because it helps us make sense out of your behavior and as you can see, there are certain categories that you do not want to be placed in. Single men make up a lot of excuses as to way we remain single and struggle with abandoning singlehood, but the most influential factor is your behavior—you are the X-Factor.

Part Three

The Screening Guide: How Not To Waste Your Time

Chapter 9

Determine If He Can Offer Quality Time: Quality Time Is Critical

Determine if a man can offer you quality time because your time is important. What do I mean? As a therapist, I talk and listen to women daily and find out more about you all in one hour than your significant other does in five or ten years of dating or marriage. I am capable of establishing this connection with women like you because I offer quality time, not quantity. A man can buy you expensive gifts, take you out to dinner, to the movies and on a first-class trip around the world and never get to know you because he does not listen to you.

So how do you determine if you are getting quality time?

A man should be able and willing to sit down and listen to what is on your mind. A man who offers quality time has a genuine interest in trying to understand what motives and drives you. However, he can only do these things if he takes the time to ask: "How are you feeling? How was your day? How are you doing? How can I help you? Is there something I can do to make your life and our relationship better?

You should be having conversations with meaning. If you are not having interactions with meaning, than you are not necessarily getting quality time. *Quality time involves a certain level of attentiveness.* You know what you need and want from a man and he should be willing to explore and entertain your needs. I am not suggesting that a man has to devote all of his time and energy to you, but I am suggesting that he should be able to hear you out when you are in need. Believe it or not, a man who gives his time is probably more into you than a man who gives his money and material things. After all, material things and money is nothing to a man who is doing well. As Lil Wayne says, "It's not tricking if you got it."

The most precious gift that a man can offer you is quality time. Over the course of my career as therapist I have heard thousands of engaged and married women complain and become extremely frustrated because their fiancés or husbands do not spend time with them or listen to them. As I processed what they were saying to me, I learned that most women want to be heard and want attention. It is without question that we all feel better when we are heard and attended to. Therefore, I believe that quality time has to do with a man's willingness and ability to devote time to listen to you and to address your emotional needs.

Why do some women go out of their way to be noticed by men and do whatever is needed to have companionship? According to Abraham Maslow, a renowned psychologist, all humans have five basic needs: physiological, security, social, esteem and self-actualizing. Men typically address your physiological needs: water and food. Men also address your safety and security needs: protection from harm and shelter from the environment. However, of all the basic needs presented by Maslow, social needs (which include the need for belonging, love and affection) best explain why so many of you go out of your way to be noticed by men and to be swept off of your feet.

The desire to have companionship and to be accepted is an intense social need that dictates how most women behave the majority of the time. Some women will do whatever is required to get attention. Your deeply felt need to be loved, understood and accepted can best be understood by paying attention to the selfless and sometime destructive behavior that you participate in to avoid being ignored.

Once a man understands and accepts that you crave and need attention, his ability to understand and influence you will be met with less resistance. However, men must make time to nurture your needs. In most households, men work in order to address the family's physiological and security needs. And because men are consumed with addressing basic survival needs, we occasionally neglect your social need for quality time—attention and affection.

Regrettably, this universal problem affects thousands of couples on a daily basis. Men, especially those who have a strong desire to provide, usually work long hours and in some situations work two jobs in order to provide for and address their family's primary needs. As a result of being obsessed with financial security, some men believe that working is as equally important as spending time with you.

Balancing relationship and provider responsibilities can be very challenging for men. Work demands can consume a large percentage of our time. However, you should encourage men to focus on having quality interactions with you. Relationships grow when individuals address and meet each others' need for attention. Men can accomplish this task by having meaningful and quality interactions with you. Quality interactions enable both women and men to influence each others' thinking and behavior because greater understanding occurs when individuals can relate to and empathize with each other. Being a great provider and protector are great qualities, but if a man feels that he does have to spend time with you, I recommend that you exit immediately.

Steve Harvey encourages you to set some standards and men will fall in line and give you what you want—the ring. While it is important to get the ring, it is as equally important to get some quality time. In my line of work, I interact with thousands of women who have received their rings; however, a large percentage of them are not happy because they do not get quality time.

A man can give you material things, but material items do develop emotional intimacy in relationships. As a matter of fact, love and possession of material items has little impact on how individuals behave, especially if nothing is done to stimulate or nurture the love in their hearts.

How many times have you heard the saying, "Money cannot buy love?" Do you agree with this saying? I do! Unfortunately, wealthy couples experience just as much hardship and tension in their relationships as do middle class and poor couples because true companionship requires emotional bonding that occurs through meaningful interactions—quality time, not by giving or receiving material items. If a man cannot offer you quality time, do not waste your time.

Chapter 10

Assess His Emotional Availability

Assess whether or not a man is available emotionally. When he tells you that he is not looking for a serious relationship, bells should ring and you should move quickly to remove yourself from the situation. Do not enter into a relationship with an emotionally unavailable man thinking that you are going to change him. Some men will tell you where they are at emotionally and some will not. With this in mind, it is imperative that you learn how to identify, assess and walk away from men who are not emotionally available. Believe me it will save you a lot of heartache.

Identifying Emotionally Unavailable Men

There are three categories that emotionally unavailable men fall into: 1) those who are emotionally unavailable by choice; 2) those who are emotionally unavailable because they are afraid of being hurt or vulnerable; and 3) those who are emotionally unavailable by choice due to fear.

By Choice: Men who choose not to be available emotionally are frequently consumed by desires to pursue and achieve career goals. Their decision to remain emotionally unavailable is significantly influenced by their decisions to focus on their careers or other areas of their lives. They understand and are okay with putting their personal lives on the back burner and make it known that they are not available.

Fear: Men who are afraid of being emotionally available do not make a conscious choice; they are driven out of fear of being vulnerable or being hurt. They desire to be in relationships, but their fear consumes them. They desperately want and believe in companionship, but are scared as hell to go get it. Men who are afraid cope with their fear by putting their professional life in the forefront.

By Choice due to Fear: Some men make themselves emotionally unavailable by choice due to fear. This category of men desire to be in relationships, but choose to remain single out of fear. They are typically financially comfortable or stable and their careers are on track. They will talk about commitment, but will not take serious steps toward committing.

I identified three categories because I want you to understand that the reasons men give for being emotionally unavailable really do not matter because they all have devastating effects. Some of us believe that choosing to be emotionally unavailable due to career aspirations is more acceptable and manly than operating out of fear. Often we will tell you that we are focused on our careers or other issues, but a large percentage of men, in my opinion, are emotionally unavailable due to fear.

Assessing Men's Emotional Availability

If you listen to men talk about their past relationships, most will share stories about women who have either directly or indirectly hurt them or broke their hurts. It could have been a female relative (mother, sister, etc.), close female friend or their first love. In talking with men in various professional and social settings, I have found that emotionally unavailable men typically have experienced some emotional pain and decide to remain emotionally detached in order to prevent the pain from reoccurring.

I recently had a conversation with a young lady and she asked me, "How can I determine if a man is emotionally unavailable and what should I do? What does it mean when some guys choose not to be emotionally available?" Here are the answers:

Emotional unavailability describes a man's mindset. Identifying emotionally unavailable men is fairly easy. There are five major behavioral indicators that I encourage women to pay attention to: 1) does he let his guards down or share his emotions; 2) has he been in a long-term committed relationship within the past two to five years; and 3) is he approaching or has passed the age of 35 and is still single; 4) does he spend a significant amount of time focusing on school, work or other areas of his life and is only open to companionship that meets his terms; 5) does he engage in self-serving behavior and express little concern for others' emotional needs?

If a man answers yes to one or more of the behavioral indicators listed above, then there is a high possibility that he might be an emotionally unavailable guy.

Emotionally unavailable men look, act and think like any other man, but experience difficulty in regards to entering or sustaining relationships because they are extremely sensitive to being hurt. If he becomes defensive when discussing emotions, he is probably experiencing some mild fear or anxiety.

Some emotionally unavailable men deal with fear by becoming high achievers. Also, they might get involved in heart-felt community and church activities in order to feel emotionally connected to others in some way.

What is interesting is that most emotionally unavailable men are very compassionate and thoughtful. This is where it gets tricky for you. What woman does not want a compassionate and thoughtful man? You long to be in a relationship with a compassionate and thoughtful guy and will spend your whole life looking for him.

Emotionally unavailable men are not bad individuals, they simply lack the skills needed to direct their compassion and thoughtfulness towards women, especially in intimate relationships. Limiting their love and holding back are defense mechanisms.

If you come across a man who is not emotionally available, do not waste your time, especially if he is not willing to acknowledge or meet your emotional needs (more on this in Chapter 13). Keep in mind that no relationship can blossom without emotional bonding—assess for emotionally availability by using the behavioral indicators mentioned above and move on if the man you are in interested is not available. Whatever you do, do not get caught up.

Emotional Availability
Knowledge Quiz

Let's see if you can identify the different categories of men's emotional availability. Circle the correct answer for each question. The answers are listed at the end of the quiz. Good luck.

1. "I am focusing on my career right now, but I make time for important people in my life. I like dating and believe that

women are nice to hang out with, but I usually do not disclose my inner thoughts or feelings."

Emotionally Available or Emotionally Unavailable

2. "I recently got out of a bad relationship, but I am not bitter. Things happen for a reason and I have taken time to heal. I am optimistic and feel that I am still capable of loving again."

   Emotionally Available or Emotionally Unavailable

3. "Having standards is okay, but women want too much. They must also remember that no man is perfect. Too much time is spent talking about how they feel. I want to be there for my woman, but I get tired of being sensitive."

   Emotionally Available or Emotionally Unavailable

4. "I can't be with a woman who is extremely emotional. Subjectivity is important, but women need to get a grip."

   Emotionally Available or Emotionally Unavailable

5. "I have been hurt before and now I have a list of conditions women meet before I let my guard down. I am afraid of getting hurt so my future wife will have to work hard to win me over."

   Emotionally Available or Emotionally Unavailable

6. "Often we fail to realize that relationships should be built on love and respect, not perfectionist tendencies. It does not make sense to withdraw or limit love because you are not happy. Life and relationships are filled with ups and downs, but mutual respect and understanding can help."

   Emotionally Available or Emotionally Unavailable

7. "Men should strive to love their women despite their shortcomings. I want to be with a woman who will also hear me out and accept my shortcomings. I feel whole when I have a woman who encourages and wants me to express my emotions."

   Emotionally Available or Emotionally Unavailable

8. "If I tell a woman that I am focused on others areas in my life, she should not get upset. If I make it and become successful, she will benefit as well."

   Emotionally Available or Emotionally Unavailable

9. "I enjoy spending time with my woman. I do not always understand her feelings, but I try to demonstrate empathy. I listen and share my emotions and thoughts about the situation."

   Emotionally Available or Emotionally Unavailable

10. "I grew up in a household where no one expressed how they felt. Doing things for each other was more important than sitting around talking about feelings. My wife wants me to listen to her when she is sad. I would prefer to take her out. I don't do well with the feely stuff. "

    Emotionally Available or Emotionally Unavailable

For answers, see next page

Quiz Answers

1. Emotionally Unavailable
2. Emotionally Available
3. Emotionally Unavailable
4. Emotionally Unavailable
5. Emotionally Unavailable
6. Emotionally Available
7. Emotionally Available
8. Emotionally Unavailable
9. Emotionally Available
10. Emotionally Unavailable

Chapter 11

Pay Attention to Who and What Influences Him: That's His Life Line

Take note of who and what influences a man. If you are with a man and he tells you that he wants to commit to and potentially marry you, but most of his friends are single and he continues to hang-out with those guys and runs to the clubs or wherever he goes, then you really want to pay attention to the crowd that he is running with. This is important because single men typically do not transition into married life by hanging out with single men. Some people might not agree with me, but I truly believe that men who are looking to get married have to change their environments and reduce the frequency and time they spend hanging out with single men, especially if they are not commitment-minded men.

Who Influences Him

A man's social circle can tell you a lot about him. You probably agree that most of us hang out with people who are usually representatives of who we are. If a man does not disclose much information about himself, pay close attention to the behavior of men who he considers to be his good buddies.

Women often tell me that they do not find out about their men until they have dated them for an extended period of time or until they are living together. This occurs because most women do not know what to pay attention to.

If you pay attention to and take note of how a man interacts with and responds to the influential people in his life, you can get a very good understanding of how he is likely to act in a relationship. Consider Amy's story below:

> When I first met Randy I knew we would not have any problems entering into and sustaining a relationship because he was a good guy who respected women. However, after several dates I started to see Randy's true colors emerge. Randy never did or said anything that personally concerned me when we were alone, but I noticed that he responded to and treated me differently when he was around Lance, his best friend from childhood. Lance was nice to me, but he did not think highly of women in general. Lance had a

tendency to talk down to women and respond to them in a very hostile, negative and disrespectful manner.

I did not want to judge Randy based on Lance's behavior, but I should have paid closer attention. On the surface, Randy appeared to be totally different than Lance, but the more we hung out, I saw strong similarities. One of my girlfriends told me that Randy was not right for me because Lance had too much influence over him. Randy respected and looked up to Lance because he was a successful business man and did not take crap from women. Randy did not think that Lance was a bad guy and often became defensive whenever anyone said something negative about him. Randy enjoyed hanging out with Lance.

I should have stepped back when I heard Lance curse women out and Randy never said anything to him. At times I felt disrespected by the way Lance treated women and told Randy, but nothing was said.

I remember getting into a disagreement with Randy and he cursed me out like I was a stranger off the street. I was totally surprised because in three months of hanging out, I never heard him curse. I asked him why he talked to me that way and he told me that he is not going to take any crap from me. Initially, I did not want to believe that Randy was like Lance, but I found out the hard way. I guess the saying "birds of a feather flock together" is really true.

The purpose of sharing Amy's story is to remind you of the importance of paying an attention to the company that a man keeps. Understand that we are all by-products of our social circles and environments. If you fail to take into account a man's social circle and family dynamics, you will fail to capture a very important aspect of who he is.

Pay attention to a man's life line—individuals who motivate and inspire him (mother, father, friend, etc.). You should seriously explore this issue extensively when dealing with men, especially single men. Most of us value and find security in relationships that we have developed and maintained for many years. Individuals who are close to us play major roles in how we behave and think. With this in mind, you must pay close attention to your man's circle. If he is honest with himself and truly desires to make a change for the best, he will limit the amount of time he hangs around guys who might influence him in a negative way.

As I began to prepare myself for marriage, I reduced the amount of time I spent with other single guys. I made this decision because their minds were focused on hunting and conquering women. I realized that I had to change my life line if I wanted to make a smooth transition into marriage. This decision was not easy because I was teased by the fellows. I dealt with the teasing and stuck to my decision because I realized that I could not do the same things and expect that I would change suddenly after I was married.

Knowing a man's life line is critical. Many women do not pay attention to men's life lines or have no idea of how to extract this information from them. The five following questions will help you:

1. **If we were to get married, who would be your best man?**

This person is important to him and has probably been a part of his life for some time. This is someone he cares about and will probably turn to in the future. Get to know this person.

2. **Who is the most important person in your life?**

It's important to sort out who he feels plays a major role in his life. This person will definitely provide input regarding issues in your man's life.

3. **Do you have a mentor?**

Check to see if he has a mentor: a professional mentor or personal mentor. This individual will also give him advice. Most women underestimate the role that mentors play in men's life. We are more prone to listen to men who we believe are wise.

4. **Who do you go to when you need advice about relationships?**

Make sure that you know who he considers to be a relationship guru. This person will typically provide him with information about relationship issues.

5. **How would you manage a conflict between your future wife and the most important person in your life?**

This question is critical because it will help you understand where you stand in regards to the most important person in his life. This question will also give you an idea of the kind of influence the person has over your man.

Asking the abovementioned questions are critical to assessing a man's life line. If you decide to enter a relationship and do not pay attention to a man's life line, you will pay for it later. If you are bothered by a man's life line and he does not feel a need to address or respond to your concerns, do not waste your time—exit immediately.

What Influences Him

Do you have a tendency to date men who are strongly influenced by success, money, financial stability, titles, material items or fame? In our society most men are influenced by these things and women love to date men who are driven and ambitious. However, many of you fail to understand that men who are influenced by the things listed above are more likely to struggle in their relationships, especially if they do not know how to balance their lifestyles.

There is nothing wrong with dating a man who is influenced by success, money, financial stability, titles, material items or fame, but know that you will likely have problems if he is not also strongly influenced by the desire to have a healthy relationship or family. Through intimate conversations, you can get a good idea of whether or not a man's values are consistent with yours. I often suggest that women develop a list of values and rank them.

The list could include the following values: a) financial stability; b) success; c) hard work; d) honesty; e) helping people; f) healthy relationships; g) health; h) material items; i) mutual respect; j) education and k) emotional support. After developing your value list you should compare them to the man that you are interested in dating. See example below.

Your Values	Your Man's Values
1. Helping	1. Financial Stability
2. Relationships	2. Success
3. Hard work	3. Hard work
4. Honesty	4. Health
5. Health	5. Honesty

6. Success	6. Helping
7. Financial Stability	7. Relationships
8. Material items	8. Material items

Rank your values from the most to least important:

Your Values	Your Man's Values
1.______________________	1. ______________________
2.______________________	2. ______________________
3.______________________	3. ______________________
4.______________________	4. ______________________

If your values are significantly different than the man you are interested in as reflected in the example above, you should seriously consider moving on.

You must remember that the things or values that influence a man before he commits to you will also influence him after he commits to you. So make sure that your values align with the men you date. If you find that you do not like who and what influences your man, do not waste your time—remain firm in your beliefs and exit immediately.

Chapter 12

Explore His Source of Motivation: Internal or External

Explore whether a man is internally or externally motivated to be in a relationship. In working with hundreds of men over the years, I have learned that men's decision to enter into relationships stems from to two sources of motivation: internal and external. Understanding whether a man is internally or externally motivated, is the first step in determining if he is ready for a relationship. Once you identify a man's source of motivation, you will be better equipped to determine if he is worth your time. Furthermore, you will learn how to respond to him appropriately.

External Motivation

Unfortunately, large percentages of men decide to enter into relationships or get married because of external motivation. External motivation is based on societal and interpersonal influences. A man who is externally motivated is more likely to commit to you because society tells him that he has reached the point of where he should settle down and get married. External motivation may also develop from being pressured by family members and friends who feel that a man should be married.

Identifying Men Who Are Externally Motivated

Externally motivated men see the value of relationships through the eyes of others. They speak about relationships from a second person point of view. Identifying externally motivated men is critical because you do not want to end up in a relationship with a man who married you because he felt pressured or was strongly influenced by others. Make sure you do not get involved with men who are praise-seekers. Here are some typical psychological and behavioral characteristics of externally motivated men:

1. Likes to please people, especially individuals who are close to them or have influence over them.

2. Lacks internal enthusiasm and motivation.

3. Engages in behavior that others think is best for them.
4. Has difficulty saying no or speaking up when under pressure from others.
5. Looks forward to receiving praises and awards for their decisions or behavior.

You want to avoid men who are externally motivated at all costs. They are the kind of guys who disapprove of serious relationships or marriage but will enter into relationships because they desire to have women cater to their needs. Also, externally motivated men are more likely to select women based on their physical attributes or status, rather than their personalities.

Internal Motivation

Internal motivation is based on a man's self-reflective understanding that he has conquered his fear and he is ready to love you. He has made a decision to be emotionally available and is willing to give his all. Internal motivation comes from a man's personal drive and self-growth. His decision to commit to or marry you is influenced by his desire to achieve self-actualization. He understands that committing to you is the right thing to do and is driven internally to do so. An internally motivated man will commit to you because he enjoys what commitment means and offers. He does not look for external praise or awards.

Identifying Men Who Are Internally Motivated

Internally motivated men see the value of relationships through their own eyes. They speak about relationships from a personal point of view. Identifying internally motivated men is critical because you want to end up in a relationship with a man who married you because he felt personal enjoyment by being with you. Here are some typical psychological and behavioral characteristics of internally motivated men:

1. Listens to those who are close to him, but makes decisions based on personal fulfillment and needs.

2. Thrives off of internal enthusiasm and motivation.

3. Engages in behavior that they feel is best for them.

4. Does not struggle with saying no or speaking up when under pressure from others.

5. Does not need praise or awards to feel good about their decisions or behavior.

You want to invest time in men who are internally motivated. They are the kind of guys who will enter into serious relationships or marriage because they see the value in doing so and are driven from within. Also, internally motivated men are more likely to select women based on their personalities and intrinsic motivation, rather than their physically attributes or status.

Exploring the two sources of motivation is very important when trying to determine if you should waste your time on a man. Understanding motivation is vital because it provides information about why men behave the way we do. By understanding a man's motivational source you can gain insight into how he will likely achieve or accomplish his goal to enter into a serious relationship or marriage.

Motivation serves as a man's incentive to act or react in a certain way. If you are interested in being with a man who will give his all in a relationship regardless of whether or not he is being praised or pressured from others, then you definitely want to date a man who is internally motivated. As mentioned previously, you want to avoid men who are only interested in being serious or committed to you because they like to receive praise or feel pressured. This group of men is difficult to interact with and I would advise you to not waste your time—exit immediately because you will not be able to sustain their attention.

Chapter 13

Help Thy Man: Agree to Attend Professional Counseling

If He Refuses, Then What?

From my observations, I have found that women are more likely to fight when experiencing fear or emotional distress associated with relationship difficulty. In contrast, men are more likely to flee when experiencing fear or emotional distress associated with relationship difficulty. Ninety percent of the marital or consultation inquiries I receive are initiated by women. Men typically do not feel comfortable seeking help and often minimize the role that fear or emotional distress plays in their relationship difficulty. I point this out because you need to understand that any man who struggles with fear and is not willing to seek help will not be able to give you what you want—a healthy and committed relationship.

Nevertheless, I encourage women to support their men by agreeing to attend professional counseling because I believe that men should not be punished or abandoned due to experiencing fear or emotional distress if they are willing to get help. Also, I encourage women to support their men by attending professional counseling because there are benefits that they can reap.

Benefits of Attending Professional Counseling

The ability to succeed in relationships does not occur without some form of professional counseling or guidance. Even the most nurturing, self-driven and productive women require guidance and seek advice from time to time. Based on the fact that relationships can be stressful at times, it is imperative to seek help when warranted. Women and men who have healthy relationships do not solely rely on their own knowledge as the gold template, but also seek knowledge from others as they endeavor to develop and sustain healthy and productive relationships.

Benefit # 1: You can gain a better understanding of your man's fear or emotional distress.

Psychotherapists such as myself are skilled at assessing and treating men who suffer from fear or emotional distress associated with commitment. If you would like to do right by your man and yourself, you should learn about human behavior and development from a professional. Seeking counseling can eliminate the need to play mind games with an unpredictable or emotionally distraught man. Can you imagine what your relationship with your man would be like if you secured proper knowledge and combined it with your love?

By attending professional counseling you can help your man develop a plan for coping with his fear or distress. Through education and training, you can be taught to validate how your man feels, learn to communicate effectively with him, and find out how to help him apply fear reducing techniques such as Systematic desensitization and Flooding.

Benefit # 2: If you decide to remain with your man you can learn to be more empathic toward him.

By attending professional counseling you can learn how to be more empathic toward your man. Learning to be empathic is very important because most men's fear or emotional distress is associated with lack of trust in women or their inability to cope with vulnerable emotions. You can help your man cope with his fear or emotional distress by being empathic. As you model empathy, you can help your man identify and process his fear in a healthy manner.

The most effective method for understanding men's behavior and minimizing fear is to establish empathic relationships where they feel emotionally safe. Empathy is one of the most important interpersonal skills you can help your man learn. Men who learn and apply empathy are more likely to be open-minded and transparent. Creating such a relationship with men can be challenging at times, especially when you are frustrated or feel discouraged. Demonstrating empathy toward a man who is emotionally detached and cold can be tough. Occasionally, you might feel like you are wasting your time; however, you must remember that failure to demonstrate empathy toward your man can cause him to believe that you do not have his best interest at heart. ***Translation**: He will not trust you.*

For most men, the desire to be respected, valued, and supported strongly influences how we behave. Therefore, your primary goal as a woman is to help your man feel safe enough to discuss and express his fear or emotional distress with you. As you strive to become an empathic support system for your man, I am confident that you will develop a stronger emotional connection with him.

Considering and attending professional counseling is important and can prove to be beneficial to you and your man. Do not continue to struggle unnecessarily. You should consistently try to learn as much as you can about your man and develop a better understanding of what is needed to have a healthier relationship with him. This means that you should utilize all available resources.

By attending professional counseling you will significantly enhance your ability to understand, influence and connect with your man. Your dedication and commitment to obtaining knowledge will pay off if you decide to remain with him. In the end, your relationship with your man will flourish and an abundance of happiness and harmony will follow. I do not believe that a woman should walk away from her man if he has potential and is willing to grow. We all have shortcomings and should be supported if we are making genuine efforts to improve. Walking away should only happen, in my opinion, when a man refuses to help himself.

As stated previously, you cannot help or support someone who does not want to be helped or supported. It is important to be mindful of the fact that a man will not change unless he wants to. So do not think that you change a man who does not want or desire help. You can support your man and ask him to attend professional counseling, but if he refuses, then what? Exit immediately.

Chapter 14

REAL TALK with Dr. Buckingham Questions and Answers about Men and Relationships

On a yearly basis, I provide individual therapy and consultation services to hundreds of single women who are from different regions and cities around the world. Their backgrounds and experiences are very different in many ways and their views about men and relationships vary significantly; however, I am asked some of the same questions about men and relationships over and over again. Please allow me to share their questions and my answers with you.

1. Are all single men damaged emotionally and should I avoid them at all cost?

No, all single men are not emotionally damaged. In my opinion emotionally damaged men are very vindictive in nature and have intense hatred for women. Emotionally damaged men are more likely to fight dirty and will do things to intentionally hurt you. I know a lot of single men who have trust issues occasionally check out emotionally and are somewhat selfish, but I do not consider them to be emotionally damaged. You should avoid single men who solely blame women for their heart pain. Accountability is important.

2. Are all single good men arrogant, selfish and overly confident?

No, I socialize with a number of single good men that are humble, down-to-earth, have nice jobs and are looking for women who can complement them. Their decisions to be selective does not always equate to arrogance and selfishness. It is not wrong for man to desire to be with a woman who complements him. Confident men typically do not do well in relationships with women who have self-esteem issues. No man wants to consistently give a woman compliments if she does not believe them. Compatibility is critical and should be present on several levels—spiritually, emotionally and behaviorally.

3. Are all single good men superficial?

No more than you are. In some form or fashion we are all superficial. How many times have you decided not to talk to a man because of his initial conversation, income, height, weight, clothing, shoes or overall physical appearances? Men and women typically see first and act second. We do not usually take the time to get to know the opposite sex if they are not appealing to the eye first. Like you, most men are wired to focus on things that really do not matter.

4. Why do men place conditions on how they love?

Most single men place conditions on how we love in an effort to maintain control of ourselves and our relationships. Men have a strong need to be in control. Being in control empowers us to master our destiny and minimizes our risk of being vulnerable. Without displaying vulnerability, we avoid the risk of being hurt. Men are motivated by receiving love, but the fear of pain, suffering and disappointment intensifies our need to place conditions on how we love.

5. Does a man's background and upbringing impact his view of women and relationships?

Yes, definitely. As a young boy I did not understand the worth of a woman. I was not educated or informed. No man ever taught me to respect a woman or appreciate her. I grew up viewing women negatively. I thought all women were weak because they did things that nobody else would do and supported men who did not support them or stay with them. My mother birthed eight children and practically raised us by herself. I remember having mixed feeling about my mother as a young child. I loved her wholeheartedly for taking care of me, but I was also angry with her. I never expressed my emotions or concerns to my mother, and as a result, I never understood her.

At a young age I held a negative view of women, especially Black women. Witnessing the hardships and pain of my four sisters also compounded my ambivalence and negativity. They had children at early ages and engaged in activities similar to those of my mother: up-and-down relationships and raising their children alone. Only one of my sisters married, but this did not last long. Growing up and observing the hardships experienced by the women I cherished and loved was emotionally devastating. However, due to a lack of knowledge and respectful male role models, I grew up treating women the same way I saw men treat my mother and sisters (I explain how I dealt with this in my book: "*A Black Woman's Worth*: *My Queen and Backbone*").

6. How important is it to share similar core values with a man?

It is extremely important to share similar core values with a man. Similarities set the stage for intimate relationships to develop. Individuals who appear to share similar interests and beliefs are more likely to enter into an intimate relationship. However, dissimilarity in core values will cause conflict. I have provided counseling to hundreds of couples who were troubled because they did not share similar core values about communication, money management, expression of emotions and other issues that affect the quality of relationships. Interpersonal similarities are needed to develop a relationship, but similar core values are needed to sustain it. Value differences are either unrecognized or ignored in the beginning of most relationships because individuals believe that value differences should not be problematic for individuals who are deeply in love. Well these differences can be problematic.

Make sure that your core values are compatible with the any man that you are interested in. No other social institution is affected by the lack of similarities in core values like the institute of marriage. The best marriages have two individuals who are dedicated to working and developing similar core values—integrity, honesty, trust and mutual respect.

7. Why do men play games in relationships?

If a man feels that he cannot be himself in a relationship, he will send a representative who is flawless. However, if he feels that he can be himself, he will not send a representative, but will show up with his flaws visible. Men play games sometimes because we do not trust that you will accept us as is. There is a lot of pressure on men and some of us simply do not know how to handle the pressure. Game playing can be costly both financially and emotionally and definitely ruins relationships. You can alleviate some of the game playing by being honest, respectful and demonstrating acceptance of a man's shortcomings.

8. How can I help restore a man's trust in women, especially in me?

Demonstrate compassion and do not judge him. Be consistent in your words and behavior because trust is earned over time and through action. If he feels that you have compassion for him, he is more likely to demonstrate compassion for you. If he truly believes that you have his best interest at hand and will not intentionally hurt him, he will be more likely to allow himself to fall in love, thus giving up the ability to control his heart.

9. How can a man hurt me if he loves me?

You must realize that love in and of itself is not enough to prevent a man from hurting you. Human beings were created out of love to love, but we allow our emotions to distort that love. I suggest that you look at the intent of a man's heart. I have learned that good hearted men say and do bad things when their feelings are hurt. As a result, you should try to pay close attention to a man's underlying motives. If you detect that he is hurting you because he lacks insight as to how to express his emotions appropriately, provide support, guidance and pray. Basically, you should stick with him. If you detect that he is deliberately hurting you to be spiteful, you should seek professional help if warranted, provide support, guidance and also pray. If the deliberate behavior continues, you should simply remove yourself from the relationship.

10. If I love a man enough will and can he change?

Love without work does not last. I believe in the power of love, but I also believe in the power of work. You can love a man until you are blue in the face, but if he is not willing to or has no desire to change, he will not. Love is an emotion that influences the heart, not controls it. Men will and can change if we want to and showing love to us can help move the process along.

11. Where do men learn how to love?

Our first example of how to show and express love in relationships comes from family interactions. Through direct involvement or observation we learn certain skills and habits, including how to love. Most men think we love the way we do based on our personal experiences alone, but this is not true. We have all been impacted by family experiences in some form or fashion. The processing of learning how to love is strongly influenced by the adults who raise us.

12. Do men get offended when women inquire about their income or money making potential?

Yes! I can't tell you the number of times I have interacted with women who have placed more emphasize on my money making potential than on my personal qualities. Men understand that personality does not pay bills, but we also understand that money and status cannot ensure or buy love. Take the time to get to know us before you size us up financially. We understand that we have to provide for you, but we also want to feel like you are invested in us, not our wallets.

13. Does setting or establishing standards really work?

Yes and no. You can establish all kinds of standards, but a man will not change unless he wants to. Many of you get advice that suggests you should do this and you should do that in order to entrap or keep your man. Take heed, it does not matter what you do. For every behavior that you engage in order to entrap a man, he has an escape plan. Remember, I told you that men are skilled at psychological warfare. You can try to think like a man, but it will not and does not work. As a matter of fact, you should think like a lady and act like one. Quit playing games. Healthy relationships are built on effective and honest communication, self-reflection and self-growth. If you have to play mind games with a man by thinking like him, then you should not be with him.

14. How can I tell if a man is insecure or secure about being in a relationship?

This may be challenging for you, but it is fairly easy to spot insecure men. One effective way to find out if a man is insecure is to pay attention to how emotionally aroused he becomes when he speaks about commitment and relationships. If a man speaks about commitment and relationships with excitement, openness, optimism and eagerness, he is probably secure in his identity. However, if a man speaks about commitment and relationships with boredom, caution, pessimism and apathy, he is probably insecure.

15. Do emotionally unavailable men care about women?

Yes, they do care about women, but they care about themselves more. At the end of the day, when a man chooses to interact with and lead you on, regardless of the understanding you all have, he is being selfish, especially if he knows that you want more. Caring means letting go!

16. Are men stronger than women?

Most women and men would agree that men are typically stronger than women from a physical standpoint; however, when it comes to dealing with emotions that is a different story. When women get hurt you all mourn for a short period and move on after actively coping with your pain. Men on the other hand, will often allow heartbreak and trauma to fester and lead to emotional roadblocks that hinder our ability to move on.

17. Do single men avoid marriage and commitment because they are afraid of taking on more responsibility?

Some do and some don't. I believe that a large percentage of men do not mind the responsibility that comes along with being the head of a household because we expect to do that. Most men are afraid to rely on women for emotional support and comfort. Also, single men take pride in and are used to being self-reliant.

18. How can I tell if a man lusts after me or loves me?

Unfortunately, women and men have confused lust with love without realizing that they operate in opposition to each other: If a man truly loves you he will wait to be married before having sex if that is what you desire; if he lusts after you he will pressure you to jump in the bed before marriage. If a man loves you, he will appreciate your mind; if he lusts after you he will appreciate your body (I explain the difference between love and lust in my book, *Unconditional Love: What Every Woman and Man Desires in A Relationship*).

19. What are the chances of a man marrying in his late thirties?

Not good. Most men who are really serious about marriage typically find a wife before they hit thirty. Men who are 35 years old and older are more likely to remain single, although they might express a desire to get married. Nothing is etched in stone, but research shows that men who are 35 and older typically do not marry.

20. Can single men live pleasurable lifestyles alone?

"Pleasurable lifestyle" is a subjective term, but I believe so. I know a lot of single guys who live good lives and appear to be satisfied with their lifestyles. They find pleasure in accomplishing career goals, traveling and doing things they enjoy doing. In regards to having and wanting companionship, many of them are open to marriage, but do not feel a need to rush into it. I hate to say it, but companionship can be bought. A man who is not looking for a serious relationship is okay with spending money on women for personal gain.

21. Can single men refrain from having sex for extended periods?

Yes, I am a living example. I have been abstinent for the past 4 years. And believe me I am not gay and nothing is medically wrong with me. Some men do grow up and start using our big head more than we use our little head. I took some time to get myself together. After years of going through drama, I decided to stop having sex with women. This was not easy, but I learned a lot about myself and women after I stop sleeping with you all. I learned that I am disciplined and learned that women who respect their bodies cannot give themselves without wanting more. I refrained by not putting myself in risky situations—no opportunity, no sex.

22. This guy keeps telling me that he loves me, but is not in-love with me. What the hell does that mean?

Over the past fourteen years, I have heard hundreds of men tell women they love them, but are not in love with them. I started to inquire about the meaning and kept notes. After reviewing my notes and discussing this with men, I came up with the following explanation: when a man tells a woman he loves her, he means that he cares about her deeply and would never want anything to happen to her. He views her as someone who is special. He distinguishes love from being in-love by detaching emotionally. When he says that he is not in-love, he is saying that he does not feel attached to you on an emotional level—he does not feel spiritually or intimately attached.

23. Do men like women with masculine tendencies?

Excuse my French, but hell no. Being independent and successful is totally different than being masculine. No man wants a woman who acts just as aggressively as he does. I know this does not sound fair, but men are attracted to and want a woman who is feminine on many levels. The quickest way to turn a man off is to start acting tough and insensitive. I often encourage women not to let men take them outside of their lady zone—the place where you feel most comfortable.

24. Why do some women choose to date or get involved with emotionally unavailable men?

I have found that women who lack understanding of their worth typically get involved with emotionally unavailable men. Most of them suffer from low self-esteem. On the other hand, desperation can play a major role. I have worked with some very confident and strong women who have found themselves in these kinds of relationships because they felt that their options were limited—struggling with the "a good man is hard to find" issue.

25. What can a woman do to break off a fling or relationship with an emotionally unavailable man?

Stop spending time with him. Minimize and eventually cut off all contact. I would suggest that you do this slowly so that you do not experience intense emotional withdrawal. If you pull back too soon the withdrawal might be too much for you to handle and you will keep going back. Develop a withdrawal plan or contact me—smile.

26. Should I give into dating men who do not meet my standards?

No, please stick to your standards. I say this because it is not fair to you or the man if you lower your standards. Settling is never good because you will always have a yearning for what you think you are missing. If you like a man with a certain build, look or intellect you should date men who meet your criteria. Be careful when dating men who do not meet your criteria...love will and can creep up on you and before you know it you are in a relationship and unhappy. However, if you end up in a relationship with a man who does not meet all of your standards, learn to love him unconditionally and keep your hands and eyes off other men.

27. Is rebound love and dating bad for me?

Yes! Some of your girlfriends might tell you that the easiest way to get over a man is to get with another one. This is bad advice. Please allow your heart to heal so that you do not enter into another relationship with unresolved emotional baggage. Also, if you move too quick you might end up in another bad relationship. Remember that good things come to those who wait and heal properly.

28. I am not good at identifying men who do not have my best interest at hand. How can I improve in this area?

Contact me!

29. Should I date casually so I can get better at screening men?

Some people say that practice makes perfect, but it depends on what you mean by casual dating. In this day and age, men and women view dating differently. If you decide to engage in this behavior, I highly recommend that you make it clear what your intentions are. This could be helpful if you have not ventured on-to the dating scene much. By meeting different men you can get an idea of what you like and do not like. Be careful though be-cause you can get caught up. You might find that you like some qualities in one man and some qualities in another man.

30. Do married women suffer more than single women when relationships do not work out?

Not necessarily. What most people fail to realize is that a piece of paper does not determine how a person feels about or copes with heartbreak, love or commitment. I have provided counseling to thousands of single women and men who have ex-perienced just as much pain and distress in their relationships as married women. The difference is not emotional in nature, but legal. Married women often feel trapped when things do not work out, but so do single women who have children and other obligations with their counterparts.

31. What will increase my chances of entering into a healthy relationship a man?

Acquiring knowledge and seeking professional guidance is the key to having healthy relationships, so please do not depend on your experience alone. Vernon Law, a famous baseball player, once stated, "Experience is a hard teacher because she gives the test first and the lesson afterwards." Instead of feeling frustrated and discouraged on a daily basis, try equipping yourself with proper knowledge so that you can be adequately prepared for the test—dealing with an unpredictable man.

It is unfortunate that one of the most important aspects of life –developing healthy relationships– is a task that many women believe can best be accomplished through experimentation and practice. In others areas of your life, where you are responsible for others, you are required to study and acquire knowledge before you can perform those tasks. For example, before you can secure your driver's license, you must study the examination book and pass the test. This process was put into place and is enforced to ensure that you do not harm yourself or others when you get on the bi-ways and highways. Why is there no process or plan in place that requires women and men to secure knowledge before entering into relationships?

32. Do women check out emotionally? If yes, what's different from men?

Yes! I have met plenty of women who are emotionally unavailable for a various reasons (busy, focused on career, rebounding from painful relationship, etc.) just like men. However, women who are truly interested in having companionship tend rebound quicker than men. This happens particularly because women are emotional creatures. Also, women are more resilient than men when it comes to emotions.

33. Why do so many smart women like me fall in love or develop interest in men who do not truly care about us?

Unlike men, you allow your emotions to guide you. You accept emotions and release them. Men on the other hand, have been raised to hide and repress emotions. Falling in love is an emotional process for most women, but we men make it a logical process. Contrary to popular belief, emotions control your thinking and behavior, not intellect. Work to neutralize your emotional intensity and you will be capable of making more rational decisions about men.

34. Do men process and make decisions differently than we do?

Men and women process in similar manners, but make decisions differently. For example, both women and men process in the following manner: Think-Feel-Do; however, men typically make decisions based on what we think and women typically make decisions based on how you feel.

35. Is it healthy for men to avoid or repress their emotions?

No. A lot of men continue to have problems in their relationships because we do not know how to deal with emotions. Emotional stagnation is a major problem for men. Men who fail to deal with emotions will often drain the energy out of those around them. Given this, do not enter a relationship with a man who has no desire to improve his emotional well-being. Remember: qualifications do not mean qualified.

36. Do men feel secure and confident when they are in positions to provide for their families?

Yes and No. You are led to believe that a man will feel secure and confident once he is in a position to take care of you—this is partially true. The whole truth is this: a man's sense of security stems from his ability to address and protect his emotional well-being first and yours second. If a man feels or believes that you will or have the potential to hurt him emotionally, he will not put you first in his life. Losing money and material items hurts men, but not like heartbreak. Being able to provide for and protect you is one thing, but he will only do that if he feels safe and secure with himself.

Epilogue
Shallowness Creates Problems for Women

I cannot emphasize to you enough the importance of looking beyond a man's surface. By focusing primiarily on a man's qualifications, physical apperance, ability to provide and protect, you will never understand men or find true love.

Do not believe the hype about men being simple. Yes, we have some very basic needs, but nothing is simple when it comes to meeting them. Be careful of the words you choose to use you when you describe and interact with men—no man likes to be referred to as simple. This is very important for you to undestand because if you view men as being simple, you will treat us in a simple manner. And I can promise you that this will not turn out good for you. As I mentioned in the introduction, you should be very selective about the information you choose to receive and use. We are all guilty of making generalizations, but remember that every man is unique is his own right. Some men are more complex than others.

In conclusion, I ask that you dig a little deeper and keep the following quote in mind as you interact with men, especially qualified, yet single men.

When you meet a man, you judge him by his clothes; when you leave, you judge him by his heart.

– Russian Proverb

Food for Thought
Quotes about Love, Women and Men

Love

Love is not a feeling. Love is an action, an activity... Genuine love implies commitment and the exercise of wisdom... love as the will to extend oneself for the purpose of nurturing one's own or another's spiritual growth... true love is an act of will that often transcends ephemeral feelings of love or cathexis, it is correct to say, "Love is as love does."

– Scott Peck

Love is when you look into someone's eyes and see their heart.

– Jill Petty

A man falls in love through his eyes, a woman through her ears.

– Woodrow Wyatt

I don't want to live—I want to love first, and live incidentally.

– Zelda Fitzgerald

You know it's love when you want to give joy and damn the consequences."

– Frank Herbert

Do you love me because I am beautiful, or am I beautiful because you love me?

– Cinderella

Love doesn't make the world go round. Love is what makes the ride worthwhile.

– Franklin P. Jones

Love is an ocean of emotions entirely surrounded by expenses.

– Lord Dewar

Love is being stupid together.

– Paul Valery

You never lose by loving. You always lose by holding back.

– Barbara DeAngelis

Love is life. And if you miss love, you miss life.

– Leo Buscaglia

Love has its own time, its own season, and its own reasons from coming and going. You cannot bribe it or coerce it or reason it into staying. You can only embrace it when it arrives and give it away when it comes to you.

– Kent Nerburn

Love enables you to put your deepest feelings and fears in the palm of your partner's hand, knowing they will be handled with care.

– Carl S. Avery

Love is patient, love is kind.

It does not envy, it does not boast, it is not proud.

It is not rude, it is not self-seeking.

It is not easily angered, it keeps no record of wrongs.

Love does not delight in evil, but rejoices with the truth.

It always protects, always trusts, always hopes, always perseveres.

Love never fails.

– Corinthians 13:4-8

Women

A woman in love can't be reasonable---or she probably wouldn't be in love.

– Mae West

There are no good girls gone wrong—just bad girls founded out.

– Mae West

Good girls go to heaven, bad girls go everywhere.

– Mae West

Women always worry about things that men forget; men always worry about things women remember.

– Majorie Kinnan Rawlings

Women have wonderful instinct about things. They can discover everything except the obvious.

– Oscar Wilde

Women marry men hoping they will change. Men marry women hoping they will not. So each is inevitably disappointed.

– Albert Einstein

Men

Men are anxious to improve their circumstances, but are unwilling to improve themselves; they therefore remain bound.

– James Allen

Men are what their mothers made them.

– Ralph Waldo Emerson

Men are rich only as they give. He who gives great service gets great rewards.

– Elbert Hubbard

A man is already halfway in love with any woman who listens to him.

– Brendan Francis

Men are all alike....except the one you've met who is different.

– Mae West

A man is not where he lives, but where he loves.

– Latin Proverb

I would rather trust a woman's instinct than a man's reason.

– Stanley Baldwin

An archaeologist is the best husband a woman can have. The older she gets the more interested he is in her.

– Agatha Christie

I love the man that can smile in trouble; that can gather strength from distress, grow by reflection.

– Thomas Paine

Understanding Abuse

It is important to understand abuse. Some of you are in abusive relationships and do not know it. Love should not hurt, at least not intentionally. I hope you find this information to be helpful.

Different Forms of Abuse

- Physical Abuse (inflicting physical discomfort, pain or injury) Slapping, hitting, burning, punching, restraining, sexually assaulting, handling roughly, etc.
- Sexual Abuse (forced sexual contact, rape or incest)
- Psychological/emotional abuse (diminishing your identity and self-worth) Threatening, insulting, name calling, yelling, imitating, ignoring, isolating, etc.

- Neglect (failure to meet your needs or those of others) Inadequate physical or emotional care: denial of food, water, clothing, health care, etc.

Symptoms of Abuse — "Misuse of Power and Control"

Using Physical Abuse

- Pushed or shoved you
- Held you to keep you from leaving
- Slapped or bit you
- Kicked, choked, hit or punched you
- Locked you out of the house
- Abandoned you in a dangerous place
- Refused to help you when you were sick, injured, or pregnant
- Subjected you to reckless driving
- Forced you off the road or kept you from driving
- Raped you
- Threatened or hurt you with a weapon

Using Sexual Abuse

- Told anti-woman jokes or made demeaning remarks about women
- Insisted that you dress in a more sexual way than you wanted
- Called you derogatory sexual names like "whore" or "freak"
- Forced you to strip when you did not want to
- Forced you to have unwanted sex with others or forced you to watch others
- Forced sex after beatings
- Forced sex for the purpose of hurting you with objects or weapons
- Committed sadistic sexual acts

Using Emotional Abuse

- Put you down
- Made you feel bad about yourself
- Called you names
- Made you think you are crazy

- Played mind games with you
- Humiliated you
- Made you feel guilty

Using Male Privilege

- Treated you like a servant
- Made all the big decisions
- Acted like the "master of the castle"
- Was the one to define men's and women's roles

Using Economic Abuse

- Prevented you from getting or keeping a job
- Made you ask for money
- Gave you an allowance
- Took your money
- Didn't let you know about or have access to family income

Using Coercion and Threats

- Made or carried out threats to do something to hurt you

- Threatened to leave you, to commit suicide, to report you to welfare
- Made you drop charges
- Made you do illegal things

Using Intimidation

- Made you afraid by using looks, gestures, or actions
- Smashed things
- Abused pets
- Displayed weapons

Using Children

- Made you feel guilty about the children
- Used the children to relay messages
- Used visitation to harass you
- Threatened to take the children away

Using Isolation

- Controlled what you do, who you see and talk to, what you read and where you go

- Limited your outside involvement

- Used jealousy to justify actions

Minimizing, Denying, Blaming

- Made light of the abuse and did not take your concerns about it seriously

- Said the abuse didn't happen

- Shifted responsibility for abusive behavior

- Said you caused the abuse

Sweet Baby Syndromes (How He Gets to Come Back)

- Honeymoon Syndrome

- Super Dad Syndrome

- Revival Syndrome

- Sobriety Syndrome

- Counseling Syndrome

Common Characteristics of Battered Women

- Has low self-esteem

- Is a traditionalist about the home
- Accepts responsibility for the batterer's actions
- Suffers from guilt, yet denies terror and anger
- Has severe stress reactions with psychophysiological complaints
- Uses sex as a way to establish intimacy
- Believes that no one will be able to help her resolve her predicament

Common Characteristics of the Batterer

- Has low self-esteem
- Believes all the myths about battering relationships
- Is a traditionalist
- Blames others for his actions
- Is pathologically jealous
- Presents a dual personality
- Has severe stress reactions

- Uses sex as an act of aggression
- Does not believe violent behavior should have negative consequences

Reaction of Women Being Beaten

- Denial
- Blaming self
- Ambivalence

Long-Term Effects of Domestic Violence

- Physical
- Mental
- Economic
- Children

Abuse/Neglect Screening Questionnaire

If you answer yes to one or more of the questions below, please talk to someone you trust and/or seek help.

- Has any man ever touched you without your consent?
- Has any man ever made you do things you didn't want to do?
- Has any man taken anything that was yours without asking?
- Has any man ever scolded or threatened you?
- Are you afraid of your man?
- Are you alone a lot?
- Do you have low self-esteem?
- Do you feel like you are emotionally unstable?
- Do you feel depressed? Are you anxious frequently? Are you angry often?
- Do you feel hopelessness? Do you feel guilty? Are you sad?
- Are you overly compliant or passive?
- Are you extremely aggressive or demanding?
- Are you extremely dependent on your man?

Seek help immediately if you or a friend is being abused. Battered Women's National Hotline: 1-800-799-7233. Abuse Hotline: 1-888-743-5754.

Scheduling for Seminars or Speaking Engagements

Expanding Horizons by keeping it "R.E.A.L."

Dr. Buckingham conducts educational wellness seminars for individuals, families, groups, churches and organizations throughout the year.

"Qualified, yet Single" is one of the most requested seminars; however, Dr. Buckingham conducts seminars on a variety of topics related to ineffective communication, stress management, relationship difficulty and personal growth.

RHCS is dedicated to helping you expand your horizons!

To book an event:

R.E.A.L. Horizons Consulting Service, LLC
P.O. Box 2665
Silver Spring, MD 20915

240-242-4087 Voice Mail
www.realhorizonsdlb.com

I hope this book has been a blessing to you and I welcome your comments.

dwayne@realhorizonsdlb.com

This book can also be purchased on-line at:

www.realhorioznsdlb.com

Amazon.com

Target.com

BarnesandNoble.com

BooksaMillion.com

About the Author

Dr. Dwayne L. Buckingham is a psychotherapist and the Chief Executive Officer and Founder of R.E.A.L. Horizons Consulting Service, LLC in Silver Spring, Maryland. A commissioned officer in the United States Air Force, for nearly a decade he provided psychological assessments and treatment to over ten thousand individuals, couples, groups, and families worldwide. He is currently serving as a commissioned officer in the United States Public Health Service. Additionally, he provides individual and marital therapy to military personnel assigned to the Walter Reed National Military Medical Center in Bethesda, Maryland. Dr. Buckingham is also an active member of the National Association of Social Workers and Kappa Alpha Psi, Inc.

He is driven by the belief that every individual can improve his or her ability to cope with life challenges productively if given the opportunity and right support. Dr. Buckingham reminds individuals daily that a little understanding and education eliminates barriers and enables them to grow. He views his role as a community resiliency consultant. Through consultation and training, he hopes to provide individuals with the knowledge and skills essential to establishing and maintaining a positive and productive lifestyle.

Dr. Buckingham conducts educational wellness seminars for individuals, groups, families, organizations, and churches each year. Please visit his website at www.realhorizonsdlb.com for more information.